THE LOYALTY ADVANTAGE

ESSENTIAL STEPS TO ENERGIZE YOUR COMPANY, YOUR CUSTOMERS, YOUR BRAND

Dianne M. Durkin

AMACOM

American Management Association

New York • Atlanta • Brussels • Chicago • Mexico City • San Francisco
Shanghai • Tokyo • Toronto • Washington, D.C.

This publication is designed to provide accurate and authoritative information in regard to the subject matter covered. It is sold with the understanding that the publisher is not engaged in rendering legal, accounting, or other professional service. If legal advice or other expert assistance is required, the services of a competent professional person should be sought.

Library of Congress Cataloging-in-Publication Data

Durkin, Dianne M., 1947–
  The loyalty advantage : essential steps to energize your company, your customers, your brand / Dianne M. Durkin.
        p.   cm.
  Includes bibliographical references and index.
  ISBN 0-8144-0817-6
  1. Employee motivation.   2. Employee loyalty.   3. Organizational commitment.   4. Interpersonal communication.   I. Title.

HF5549.5.M63D87   2005
658.3'14—dc22

                                                            2004030979

Printing number

10   9   8   7   6   5   4   3   2   1

For my parents,
Irene and Joseph Michonski,
for teaching me the rules of life and loyalty.

Contents

Preface

Since 1996, Loyalty Factor, LLC, a specialized training and consulting firm dedicated to helping organizations initiate and manage change, has promoted a single, simple message—*Employee loyalty drives customer loyalty, which drives brand loyalty.*

In the last decade I have made that statement to hundreds—perhaps thousands—of individuals, in settings ranging from small meetings with prospective clients to auditoriums filled with CEOs. The reaction is always the same. People nod their heads in virtually unanimous accord.

What you will discover in reading this book is that fully embracing the Loyalty Factor requires a fundamental shift in thought and behavior, both organizationally and individually. This shift is grounded in what I have discovered—that to achieve enduring success in building brand loyalty, enterprisewide effort needs to start at the core—with core values, core competencies, and core relationships. From that core is crafted the foundation upon which organizational success and long-term profitability are built. That result is what we call the Loyalty Advantage.

The formula I describe throughout this book is neither fad, nor trend, nor flavor-of-the-week quick fix. It is a comprehensive philosophy of doing business, from the inside out.

By choosing Loyalty Factor as my business name, my philosophy is always in the room with me. It is present in all the work that my consultants and I do with our clients. It is a constant reminder of the principal focus of our work together—to develop an organizational environment that possesses a strong, positive belief in people and that sustains a triple standard—high individual performance, enduring customer relationships, and profitability over time. The Loyalty Factor culture grows out of a process that cultivates and supports continuous improvement in productivity, quality, and service.

With the loyalty-focused culture in place, customers not only choose to do business with your organization "no matter what," but also recommend you to their customers, friends, and colleagues without hesitation. When the Loyalty Factor thrives, there is a significant reduction in both voluntary employee turnover and customer defection.

There are, of course, many variables that contribute to an organization's culture. In this book I discuss those that are especially relevant to the issue of loyalty—at an employee level, a customer level, and a brand level. I present a new filter through which to assess organizational success along the way to the bottom-line goal of sustained profitability. In pursuit of satisfied employees with the capacity and willingness to drive unflappable loyalty from your customers, I offer a compendium of strategies and tactics to develop and strengthen the Loyalty Factor in your organization.

Acknowledgments

I would especially like to thank Johanna Skilling, who helped me shape my vision for this book into reality. Special thanks also to Jackie Herskovitz for her advice and counsel on this and so many other projects, and to the dedicated and hardworking team at Loyalty Factor, LLC.

My thanks as well to all those who were kind enough to help provide and review information that appears in the book, including CarePlus, Eastern Bank, Kronos Incorporated, The International Golf Club, The Timberland Company, Graniterock, Beth Israel Deaconess Medical Center, USAA, Tiffany & Co., Stellar Solutions, Griffin Hospital, The Proctor & Gamble Company, Whirlpool Corporation and KitchenAid USA, Texas Instruments, Southwest Airlines, Rackspace, Booz Allen Hamilton, The Hire Tough Group, and The Courage Institute.

Finally, thanks to Christina Parisi, Jim Bessent, and all the other talented people at AMACOM who have been my partners in bringing *The Loyalty Advantage* to you.

Introduction

When I began writing this book, a lot of people had a very similar question for me: "Is there any such thing as loyalty anymore?"

The premise on which I've built my business is that loyalty is not dead, but it's certainly been in hiding. Recent history helps us understand the many factors behind what appears to be a loss in corporate, employee, and consumer loyalty; that same history, however, gives us vital information to help us bring loyalty back into the mainstream of business.

The Loyalty Advantage is what happens when company leaders and managers create an environment in which loyalty can thrive. Companies that enjoy the Loyalty Advantage know that it creates more favorable brand perceptions among consumers and other stakeholders, and improved economic measures—including increased productivity, higher profitability, and lower employee turnover.

How do you go about creating the Loyalty Advantage in your company? This book is a step-by-step guide to do just that. In addition, you'll see examples of companies of various sizes, in industries ranging from finance to health care to outdoor wear to golf, which demonstrate that the Loyalty Advantage is available to any company, at any time. All you need to do is begin.

The heart of the process to achieve the Loyalty Advantage is what we call "the Loyalty Factor," our three-step formula to drive lasting loyalty: *Employee loyalty drives customer loyalty, which drives brand loyalty.*

The Loyalty Factor is both a *philosophy* that integrates management practices, operating systems, human resources, sales, and marketing with the company mission, vision, and values, and a *set of guidelines* that company leaders can use to bring all the constituencies of the organization to function together toward a common goal. The Loyalty Advantage—and all its benefits to the brand and bottom line—is the result.

Companies that appear on the lists of "most admired," "best to work for," and "best run" often share characteristics defined by the Loyalty Factor, including a CEO and top management team dedicated to understanding and meeting the needs of employees, customers, shareholders, and other company stakeholders. These leaders consider loyalty a fundamental part of their business vision and the foundation of business growth.

In contrast, other companies push loyalty issues down to departmental levels, where varied perspectives create different definitions of loyalty. These perspectives tend to create silos of unrelated activities:

- Marketing is charged with developing brand loyalty, which includes building the company's image and improving market share.
- Customer service measures success in terms of customer satisfaction surveys.
- Information systems provide customer data and analyses to build Customer Relationship Management strategies.
- Sales departments depend on customer loyalty to meet sales targets and gain referrals.
- Human resources measures employee loyalty in terms of reduced turnover, and the success of incentives and benefits programs.
- Shareholders measure their loyalty in dividends, and/or rising stock prices.

Relying on these unrelated procedures to create business growth leaves companies open to competition from companies that understand how integrating vision, values, and systems can—and does—create the lasting loyalty among employees, customers, and investors that leads to long-term business success.

Welcome to the Loyalty Advantage.

PART 1

WHATEVER HAPPENED TO LOYALTY?

1

Loyalty Then and Now

"Semper Fidelis."—U.S. Marine Corps

Always Faithful: That's been the motto of the U.S. Marine Corps for 120 years. According to the Marines themselves, "That Marines have lived up to this motto is proved by the fact that there has never been a mutiny, *or even the thought of one*, among U.S. Marines" (italics added).[1]

We'll leave it up to the Marine Corps to know how it can be sure that it knows every Marine's thoughts; its certainty does underscore the idea that true loyalty is a function of both *actions* and *attitudes*.[2]

Webster's defines loyalty as "unswerving allegiance," being "faithful to a private person to whom fidelity is due," or being "faithful to a cause, ideal, or custom."[3] As we'll see, those definitions of loyalty can prove to be very different in practice—and can cause conflicts on a monumental scale.

Our earliest ancestors probably learned that loyalty was a valuable survival tool. In the jungle, the desert, or the open plains, loyalty to your tribe increased your chances of surviving harsh weather and an unreliable supply of food and water.

As civilizations grew, the concept of loyalty evolved to include loyalty to one's king and country. Being loyal meant following the rules, whether those rules were the laws of the land or the whims of the king.[4] Disloyalty to national or religious ideals could be punished harshly, often by torture or execution. Even *accusations* of disloyalty became a powerful and effective weapon against perceived enemies.

The European settlers who arrived in what they called "New England" made a dramatic decision that influenced the course of history. The religious oppression that they had experienced at home had finally caused them to abandon even the pretense of loyalty to their royal rulers. Choosing instead to be loyal to God and their community, the Pilgrims gave up the material comforts of home for a voyage into the unknown and the promise of spiritual freedom.

The Pilgrims' colony in Plymouth, Massachusetts, was intended to be a communal experience; in practical terms, this meant that everyone contributed to the communal farming and labor. Enlightened self-interest, however, evolved quickly: After two years of poor harvests, Governor William Bradford decided to let each family plant its own crops. "This," he wrote, "had very good success, for it made all hands very industrious, so as much more corn was planted than otherwise would have been by any means."[5]

The Pilgrims' small experiment in rewarding individuals for their labor blossomed into thirteen thriving colonies—which famously created one of the most successful experiments in "disloyalty" in history.

The colonists' stunning inspiration was that, instead of being loyal to a monarch, a nation could be loyal to an *idea,* an idea so powerful that it propelled thirteen small colonies into one of the most powerful nations in the world. That idea, of course, is that all of us are created equal and are entitled to life, liberty, and the pursuit of happiness.

In our recent history, life and liberty have been unquestioned rights for all law-abiding citizens. The pursuit of happiness, however, is often subject to interpretation; the definition changes over time and is affected by politics, technology, economic and social movements, and sometimes just plain old bone-weary exhaustion.

Still, Americans are addicted to the pursuit of happiness, and our loyalties follow. As we'll see, however, happiness means different things to different people at different times. Understanding this is the first step toward understanding how leaders can cultivate loyalty that lasts.

Loyalty and Power

> *"The labor of a human being is not a commodity or article of commerce."*[6]
>
> —THE 1914 CLAYTON ACT

For most of the twentieth century, business leaders generally failed to see any need to cultivate their employees' loyalty. Like the kings of Europe, most top executives saw loyalty as something that they deserved, but that they didn't need to reciprocate: It was something that flowed up from the ranks, not down from the leaders.

As a result, workers had few rights or privileges. Until the late 1800s, there was no such thing as an eight-hour day, and employee benefits were sporadic and at the discretion of the employer. Members of the National Association of Manufacturers, for instance, spent several years discussing whether to offer health insurance to workers but concluded in 1916 that health insurance would be a "costly experiment" with no measurable results "practicable for American industry."[7]

Instead, business leaders preferred supporting private charities (at their discretion) to provide care for workers who became sick, injured, or too old to work.

Labor leaders convinced Congress that workers needed an advocate, and in 1913, the U.S. Department of Labor was created to protect and extend the rights of workers.[8,9] Today, employee benefits are seen as a tool to create employee loyalty. But in fact, what we think of as minimally acceptable benefits did not arise from corporate largesse but were legislated by the federal government.

In the midst of the Great Depression, when unemployment was over 25 percent and total wages plummeted from $50 billion to $30 billion,[10] Franklin Roosevelt emphasized the importance of the government's loyalty toward its citizens. In his 1934 Message to Congress, Roosevelt explained:

> *Security was attained in the earlier days through the interdependence of members of families upon each other and of the families within a small community upon each other. The complexities of great communities and of organized industry make less real these simple means of security. Therefore, we are compelled to employ the active interest of the Nation as a whole through government in order to encourage a greater security for each individual who composes it. . . . This seeking for a greater measure of welfare and happiness does not indicate a change in values. It is rather a return to values lost in the course of our economic development and expansion.*[11]

In the 1930s, the government created a number of new protections for employees, including such national social programs as social security, unemployment compensation, workers compensation, and a federal minimum wage and hours law. Other initiatives included recognition and protection for unions and union members, and the federal Occupational Safety and Health Act, which authorized the secretary of labor to establish health and safety standards for the workplace.

As a result of government intervention, workers no longer had to offer their employers unconditional loyalty. The law was slowly giving employees a stronger hand, and although a resulting change in the loyalty equation wouldn't be evident for a number of years, the seeds had been planted.

Loyalty to the Norm: A Culture of Conformity

After World War II, conformity counted. In the shadow of the Cold War, the language of loyalty was the language of politics. Fear of Communism and accusations of "disloyalty" to America cost thousands of people their jobs, their careers, their freedom, and in some cases, their lives.

The pressure to root out "disloyal" Americans led to the 1947 Federal Employee Loyalty Program, under which thousands of federal government workers were investigated and often fired for "subversion"; thirty-nine states followed suit with their employees. The House Un-American Activities Committee began a public investigation of numerous people in the entertainment industry; local communities banned books and even teachers.[12]

Political loyalty to the United States created a natural climate for corporate loyalty. It was Charles Wilson, whose career included being both president of General Motors and, later, secretary of defense under President Eisenhower, who famously said, "What's good for the country is good for General Motors, and vice versa."[13]

General Motors was a model for many American corporations. The company controlled virtually all aspects of production, employed a fixed labor force with specialized skills, and maintained a strong corporate identity. The business functioned like a well-oiled machine, and employees were a critical component. As a result, employee loyalty was both encouraged and rewarded—and those who were unlucky enough to lose their jobs were often stigmatized by the community.[14]

In his 1956 book, *The Organization Man*, sociologist William H. Whyte mercilessly examined how the changing culture rewarded conformity to corporate ideals. His analysis included a scathing indictment of America's new loyalties, as he wrote: "In our attention to making organization work we have come close to deifying it. . . . The fault is not in organization, in short; it is in our worship of it."[15]

In fact, by the 1950s, more Americans worked for large corporations or government agencies than for small businesses. There were tangible rewards: Between 1945 and 1960, the median family income almost doubled, as did the size of middle-class America itself, eventually including two-thirds of U.S. households.

Along with prosperity came children. Lots and lots of children. At the peak of the Baby Boom, in 1957, a baby was born every seven seconds. The boom resulted in a staggering 76 million people—today, over one quarter of the U.S. population.

Newly expanded and newly prosperous families also had a new form of entertainment and information. Between 1950 and 1960, television sets went from being a luxury to a standard object found in 90 percent of American homes.

TV brought America's biggest corporations into every home, along with the country's most-loved entertainers: Every night, millions tuned in to the Texaco Star Theater, starring Milton Berle, or the Colgate Comedy Hour, to watch Lewis and Martin, Abbott and Costello, Jimmy Durante, or Bob Hope.[16]

Americans had found a common language . . . and a common

lifestyle that included brands and products that were rapidly becoming as familiar as their next-door neighbors. Colgate on your toothbrush and Texaco in your tank became tangible proof of a successful home life.

The life that Americans saw on TV's new domestic comedies was also a model of conformity: middle class, middlebrow, and largely white. *Leave It to Beaver, The Donna Reed Show,* and *The Adventures of Ozzie and Harriet* were set in an almost mythical version of America in which everyone was married (to someone of the opposite sex) and children were well dressed and well behaved.[17] In these compact, self-sustaining nuclear families, men wore suits and ties and white shirts and went to an office; women wore lovely dresses and stayed home. Although it certainly didn't reflect reality, this was the vision to which America was loyal: Aspiring to the middle class was the definition of the American Dream.

From Idealism to Individualism

> *"I say to you today, my friends, that in spite of the difficulties and frustrations of the moment, I still have a dream. It is a dream deeply rooted in the American dream.*
> *"I have a dream that one day this nation will rise up and live out the true meaning of its creed: 'We hold these truths to be self-evident: that all men are created equal.'"*[18]
>
> —Dr. Martin Luther King, Jr.

The status quo didn't work for everyone. Loyalty to norms began to be challenged by those who wanted equal access to prosperity and education.

When Linda Brown was told that she couldn't attend her neighborhood school in Topeka, Kansas, because of her race, the NAACP fought back.[19] Eventually, *Brown v. Board of Education of*

Topeka came before the Supreme Court, whose famous 1954 ruling stated that "separate educational facilities are inherently unequal," and that segregated schools were unconstitutional.

About a year later, a tired Rosa Parks suddenly became tired of loyalty to the status quo as well. The civil rights movement shattered the era of conformity, inspiring other marginalized groups to stake their claims for equal rights and fair working conditions. Native Americans, Hispanics, and women all became engaged in the battle for individual rights and recognition.

Business began to feel pressure to accommodate the needs of the individual. No longer able to count on the unquestioning loyalty of the "organization man," corporations struggled to adapt their hiring, firing, compensation, and benefits policies for a newly diverse workforce.

And then there was Vietnam. And Watergate. Inspired in part by the public demonstrations for civil rights, Americans took to the streets by the hundreds of thousands to protest government actions; the conformity of the Cold War was gone forever. Those protests, of course, were led in large part by the Baby Boomers— the educated and privileged children of the postwar generation, and the next generation to enter the workforce.

Boomers learned that speaking out could affect the national debate, and even help change policy; for the vast majority, there was no retribution for protesting. The Boomers became known as the "Me" Generation, eager to follow through on their personal agendas and confident that they could continue to change the world. Their first loyalty was to themselves and their own ideas of a better future.

Is Loyalty Dead?

"Forget loyalty. Or at least loyalty to one's corporation. Try loyalty to your Rolodex—your network—instead."[20]

—TOM PETERS

As they joined the workforce, the Boomers entered a different world—a world, in part, that they'd created. The "Me" Generation was used to questioning authority and resisting loyalty to big government or big business. In the 1980s, despite occasional setbacks, the economy continued to grow, and, perhaps predictably, middle-class Boomers approached each job with an eye toward salary, benefits, and long-term career potential.

This was also the era in which increasing mobility and an increasing divorce rate began changing the family. Sexual liberation and women's greater desire to join the workforce meant that more people were staying single, or staying single longer, than in their parents' generation. Just as the migration to cities in the 1930s had eroded the traditional extended family model, the freedom of movement experienced by many Boomers began eroding ties to the 1950s "nuclear" family.

Without traditional structures, Boomers threw themselves into their jobs—and began expecting commensurate rewards. The corporation became the family, and, once again, TV reflected some of this new social reality. *The Mary Tyler Moore Show* was the first of many to depict a single person interacting solely with her colleagues and friends; family (either parents or a husband and child) was not even a small part of the picture.

While the economy continued to grow, loyalty became a matter of continued rewards in terms of advancing careers and increased compensation and perks. When the downturn came, however, it hit hard. Between the end of the 1980s and 1996, according to the consulting firm Challenger, Gray and Christmas, 3 million people were laid off.

Economic downsizing was supplemented by the increasing impact of technology, which made it possible to replace many workers with machines, especially in the manufacturing sector.[21] Jobs also began to migrate to other countries as global organizations saw opportunities to lower costs with local (and lower-paid) workers. The jobs that had formerly offered virtual lifetime employment at many companies were gone—permanently.

Downsizing was a blow not only to the wallet and the ego, but to the heart, an emotional betrayal that affected an entire generation. Employees began realizing that no matter how hard they worked, they were vulnerable: If companies were not going to be loyal, the reasoning went, there was no reason to be loyal to them. The loyalty equation changed from corporation/employee "contracts" (specific or implied) to bonds between individuals or teams.

The economic and political issues in our new century have created new layers of complexity in the relationship between employers and employees. The corporate scandals at Enron, Arthur Andersen, WorldCom, and other companies increased the country's cynicism about employer values, while resulting in the loss of hundreds of thousands of jobs.[22] Employees reacted by transferring their loyalties from their companies to their colleagues: the people they work with, team leaders, project and product groups. Layoffs are often treated like little deaths: People cry over the loss of their colleagues; bring casseroles to the homes of the newly unemployed; and are emotionally affected for days, weeks, or longer.

As the recession of 2001 took hold and deepened, employees were loyal because they had to be. Working harder and faster as employers cut more and more jobs, many people felt that they were in a grown-up, high-stakes version of musical chairs . . . and they were willing to do whatever it took to keep their chairs when the music stopped.

Today, as the economy shows signs of renewed vigor, the balance of power may once again be shifting. In a statement that says as much about the current climate as about the historic cycles of loyalty, journalist Daniel McGinn, in a May 2004 *Newsweek* article, wrote, "There may be a karmic beauty in watching bosses' power erode as the economy gives long-suffering employees new options."[23]

The Evolving Workforce

"There is a big problem looming. . . . Members of the Baby Boom generation will soon begin to retire, and there are considerably fewer workers prepared to replace Boomers in the workplace."[1]

—JERRY J. JASINOWSKI, PRESIDENT,
NATIONAL ASSOCIATION OF MANUFACTURERS

We have a math problem.

According to the U.S. Bureau of Labor Statistics (BLS), by the year 2006 there will be 151 million jobs in the country, but only 141 million people to fill them.[2] By 2031, that gap could increase to 35 million.[3]

The reason for this is rooted in demographics. Declining birthrates in the United States have led to an aging workforce: As the Baby Boomers begin to retire, the percentage of people in their prime working years, generally defined as age 25 to 54, will shrink.

The BLS predicts that by the year 2006, two employees will leave the workforce for every one who is added to it.

Overall, the numbers suggest that there will be greater competition for workers over the next decade. Depending on your industry, that competition might be heated: The BLS projects that jobs in education, health services, and professional and business services will grow twice as fast as the overall economy; other fast-growing industries include information services, leisure and hospitality, transportation, warehousing, and construction.[4] Companies that can attract and keep loyal employees will develop a competitive edge, as well as a better return on their investment in their workforce.

In its report "The Changing Face of the 21st Century Workforce," the Employment Policy Foundation says: "Faced with slower labor force growth, an aging workforce, and strong overall demand, firms must be more creative in recruiting new workers to fill job openings."

In addition to creative recruiting, companies will have to develop more creative retention strategies as well. Keeping those employees who add value and whose contributions lead to greater profitability and efficiency will require taking a closer look at the workforce and learning just what motivates it. The answer isn't always simple.

A New Diversity

> *"The next 75 years could bring continued prosperity to the American workplace. . . . However, future prosperity is not guaranteed to the American workplace, a workplace policy framework that respects diversity, encourages innovation, rewards productivity and maintains flexibility is necessary."*[5]
>
> —THE EMPLOYMENT POLICY FOUNDATION

Thirty years ago, discussions about diversity in the workplace focused on creating new opportunities for women and people of color.

Today, diversity in the workplace encompasses not just race and gender, but also religion, sexuality, family size, and other increasingly individual and personal factors. The advent of true globalization has further expanded the definition of employee diversity to people living and working in different cultures, speaking different languages, and having different legal systems and infrastructures. Outsourcing takes the diversity mix one step further by including "employees" who work for completely different companies—again, often in completely different countries and cultures.

In addition, the twenty-first century brings a new kind of diversity: age. The Baby Boomers—all 76 million of them—are for the most part still in the workforce. They've been joined by the younger generations, as well as by one surprising group: their parents. Longer, more productive working lives have changed the workplace from the typical three-generation workforce to a four-generation pool of employees that includes the so-called Veterans, Boomers, Gen Xers, and Nexters/Millennials (see Table 2-1).[6]

All of these facts underscore a simple truth: The greater the

Table 2-1. Four Generations in the Workforce

THE NEXTERS: 1978–1986

THE XERS: 1965–1977

THE BOOMERS: 1946–1964

THE VETERANS: 1922–1945

diversity of workers, the bigger the challenge of managing them. However, as we'll see, while each generation has its own distinct characteristics, there are common needs and desires that connect all the segments.

Nexters/Millennials

"From 1980 to 2000, 26.7 million new native-born workers age 25–54 provided the workforce needed for our dynamically growing economy. From now until 2021, there will be no additional native-born workers in this prime age group. None."[7]

—THE ASPEN INSTITUTE

They've been called the baby boomlet. Some 72 million strong, they began to become adults at the turn of the millennium. Like their parents, the Boomers, the Nexters make up almost a third of the population. As the most recent college graduates entering the workforce, the Nexters believe that hard work and setting goals are the route to achieving their dreams. As a result, they respond best to goal-oriented environments and leadership, especially when they understand how their work contributes to achieving the company's objectives.

Not satisfied with the slow route to the top, a majority of Nexters want to be assigned interesting and challenging work immediately; research shows that one-third of them don't feel that their skills and enthusiasm are being well utilized in their current positions. Perhaps less realistically, these young employees, sure of their skills and with an eye on their careers, want to be involved in management decision making.[8]

The Nexters consider themselves team players, but again, they don't feel that their colleagues and management reciprocate their goodwill. According to the *2002 People at Work Survey* from Mercer Human Resource Consulting, fewer than half of employees age 18 to 24 feel that they are treated fairly at work, and less than a third agree that their work group "gets the cooperation it needs from other work groups to achieve our business objectives."[9]

As a result, Nexters tend to be less satisfied with their jobs and less satisfied with their organizations than their elders, and they're not afraid to "vote with their feet." In their search for companies that they admire—and that will help them develop their careers and meet their financial needs—workers in this age group, on average, change jobs every year.[10] What helps keep them on the job? According to the AFL-CIO Working for America Institute, young workers' top concerns include:[11]

- Making sure everyone, not just the CEO, gets a fair share
- Placing more emphasis on improving education and skills training
- Having employers show more loyalty to employees who work hard

Having entered the economy at a time when money was tight, Nexters' salary expectations are not as high as those of their Gen X predecessors. They do look for nonmonetary compensation, however, and they are especially interested in job- and career-oriented education.[12] Nexters also value personal freedom, far more than older workers: According to the Mercer survey, as many as 82 percent of 18- to 24-year-olds say that flexible working arrangements are important to their job satisfaction, far more than the 58 to 69 percent of other age groups who say this. Other benefits that appeal to Nexters include tuition reimbursement, flexible spending accounts, and pet insurance; not surprisingly, they consider benefits geared toward older workers, such as retiree medical coverage and long-term care insurance, less important.

Generation X

"The older generation thought nothing of getting up at five every morning—the younger generation doesn't think much of it either."

—JOHN J. WELSH

Writer Douglas Coupland coined the term "Generation X" for the title of his 1991 first novel. That title came to stand for a disaffected "minigeneration" of slackers and nihilists—the approximately 40 million Americans born in the 1960s and 1970s.

Now in their thirties and early forties, the Gen Xers have grown up. They're adept, clever, and resourceful. They're the solid backbone of the workforce, and they're beginning to move into management positions right behind—or instead of—the Baby Boomers who came before them.

Like their younger counterparts, the Nexters, Gen X workers embody a contradiction: Independent and not given to long-term company loyalty, they are often passionate about being involved in their current jobs, and they want a dynamic, engaging, and nurturing experience at work.

Training and professional development are often key to Gen Xers loyalty and job retention; in their quest for personal fulfillment, Gen Xers especially value programs that involve mentoring, strengthening individual skills, and furthering career objectives.[13]

Like the Nexters, Gen Xers feel that benefits like these often outweigh pure financial incentives—but for somewhat different reasons. Observers, including Coupland, consistently describe Gen Xers as being somewhat less materialistic than the Baby Boomers. Whereas the Boomers, as a group, tend to "live to work," Gen Xers "work to live," valuing their time outside the office and striving to achieve a work/life balance.[14] As a result, Gen Xers appreciate such time-saving work benefits as on-site exercise facilities, ATM machines, and dry-cleaning pick-up services.

As young parents, many Gen Xers also seek out flexible work schedules and child-care benefits. It's no secret that the number of two-income families has skyrocketed. For economic reasons more than because of the "having it all" mentality of the Boomers, the women of Gen X are more likely than their predecessors to go back to work after childbirth and to continue working through their children's school years. In a significant shift from days gone by, almost three-quarters of mothers are in the labor force.[15]

Baby Boomers

"What other generation has received so much special attention?"

—HOWARD SMEAD, *DON'T TRUST ANYONE OVER THIRTY:
A HISTORY OF THE BABY BOOM*

If you ever wondered who invented the sixty-hour workweek, look no further than the Boomers. Driven to achieve even greater success than their parents, they tend to define themselves through their careers and achieve identity through the work they perform.

Roughly speaking, today's Boomers are between forty and sixty. Although their own career aspirations may have been frustrated as a result of the huge number of their peers contending for the same spots (not to mention the rising stars of Gen X), Boomers sometimes have difficulty understanding Gen Xers, who view work as a job rather than a way of life.

Financially and emotionally, Boomers are bearing the brunt of the demographic shifts that are affecting the country. Like the Gen Xers, many of them are parents of younger children as a result of delayed marriage and childbearing. But they are also the parents of the Nexters, who are in or approaching college. Even more important, because of increased longevity and better health care, the Boomers' parents are living well into their seventies, eighties, and nineties, creating brand-new issues of elder care. Not for nothing are the Boomers known as the Sandwich Generation, given their responsibilities to both the older and younger generations.

As they approach retirement age themselves, Boomers are more outwardly loyal than their younger colleagues, staying put at jobs that may offer the benefits they need. For a variety of reasons, including longer, more productive work lives, as well as, for some, the need to keep earning a paycheck, many Boomers will continue to work past sixty-five, even though they may change the kind of work they do.[16, 17]

Veterans

"You know, 60 is the new 40."[18]

—BILL MAHER

Between 1990 and 2000, the number of people age sixty-five and older increased almost 10 percent, from 32 to 35 million. By 2025, the number of seniors is expected to double, to more than 70 million.[19]

At least half of these adults are between sixty and seventy-five, a group that gerontologists call the "young old." Many Veterans are keenly aware of age discrimination and the foreshortening of their careers by the flood of Baby Boomers (ironically, their own children). As a result, while there are those who continue to work purely because of financial need, many Veterans appreciate finding work that takes advantage of their career skills (or lifelong interests) and enjoy staying productive past the traditional age of retirement.

Despite the passage of time, Veterans are still largely influenced by the organizational mentality of their youth. Educated, thorough, dedicated, and hard-working, these individuals still have a respect for authority that is fast becoming an artifact of an age gone by.[20]

Older workers also tend to stay at their jobs far longer than their younger colleagues. According to the BLS, the median tenure of workers over fifty-five is three and a half times that of workers in Gen X; 89 percent of workers over age fifty-five have been with their current employer a year or more, compared with 49 percent of Nexters.[21]

With their career achievements for the most part behind them, Veterans most appreciate recognition—not just of their contributions and loyalty to the job that they're in, but for the lives they've led. The best reward for Veterans? Respect for their life achievements as well as for their practical, intellectual, and historical skills and knowledge. Just as important are simple words or gestures of thanks—for their hard work, for their contributions to getting the job done, for helping the company achieve its goals.[22]

Of course, Veterans aren't immune to more practical incentives and motivations. Not surprisingly, health is among their chief concerns. A recent survey indicates that Veterans are very interested in such benefits as prescription coverage, health insurance, vision coverage, dental insurance, and short-term disability and paid sick days.[23]

And just like their children and grandchildren, Veterans are also interested in flexible work hours to pursue other activities; they are also actively interested in part-time and temporary work arrangements. Jobs that offer benefits have the most appeal, especially those that offer health insurance.

Managing Your Employee Portfolio

"When the only thing keeping employees on the job is fear, or golden handcuffs, those employees don't go the extra mile."

—MARC DRIZIN, WALKER INFORMATION

In addition to knowing what motivates and irritates each of these groups, it's important to understand how they work together in order to cultivate the loyalty of individuals, generational groups, and the workforce as a whole.

Each generation has different needs in terms of recognition and rewards. In addition, employers have a hidden opportunity to develop loyalty by using employees' tendency to bond with one another. Creating work teams that recognize the generations' different strengths (see Table 2-2) can both improve employees' experiences on the job and lay the groundwork for retaining valued workers when the labor market tightens.

Table 2-2. How Does Each Generation View the World?

	Veterans	Boomers	Xers	Nexters
Outlook	Practical	Optimistic	Skeptical	Hopeful
Work Ethic	Dedicated	Driven	Balanced	Determined
View of Authority	Respectful	Love/hate	Unimpressed	Polite
Leadership by	Hierarchy	Consensus	Competence	Pulling together
Relationships	Personal sacrifice	Personal achievement	Reluctant to commit	Inclusive
Turnoffs	Vulgarity	Political incorrectness	Cliché, hype	Unethical behavior

One of the best and most productive combinations is Nexters and Veterans. The Nexters appreciate many of the same values that the Veterans do, including civic duty, civic pride, dedication, morality, and achievement. Willing to learn and interested in how things have evolved from the past to the present, Nexters are a receptive audience for Veterans' stories, guidance, and reflections on how things used to be.

In return, Nexters are often able to help bring Veterans up to speed technologically. Given time and appropriate guidance, most Veterans have no trouble learning how to use everyday computers and software programs.

Each generation functions differently in larger team environments, as well. As a rule, Veterans prefer large teams with well-defined rules and roles, and a strong leader who consistently enforces the rules and agreements. Boomers, still intent on proving themselves, need to have a meaningful role on teams, if not a leadership role, or they may override what is best for the group in favor of making sure that their voice is heard. Both Gen Xers and Nexters want to understand how each challenge can help them learn and grow, and how their specific tasks contribute to a valued end result. They want well-defined, coherent goals and want to help figure out how those goals can be best achieved.

Managing your employee portfolio for maximum return in the form of loyalty requires diligence, patience, research, flexibility, and creativity.

Managing the Generations

Communicate uniquely with each generation.

Accommodate employee differences.

Create workplace choices.

Be flexible in your leadership style.

Respect competence and initiative.

Recognize achievements.

Reward results.

It's a tall order. As we'll see, the rewards of doing so are great; the risks of not doing so are tangible.

What Loyalty Means
to Business

"Loyalty shapes people's choices not only about where to work, but also about how long, hard and wholeheartedly to apply their mental energies—the fuel that drives the New Economy."[1]

—SUE SHELLENBARGER,
THE WALL STREET JOURNAL ONLINE

In industries from food service to retail to airlines, labor costs are as much as 40 percent of operating expenses.[2] With the downward shift in the U.S. economy over the past few years, U.S. companies laid off a total of almost 10 million workers.[3] That number takes on added dimension when you look at layoffs from individual companies: In some cases, the number of employees cut from a single company equals the population of a small town. In 2004, to name just a few examples, AT&T cut almost 12,000 jobs;[4] Bank of America cut about 17,000; and San Antonio–based SBC Communications, as of this writing, is considering a layoff of up to 20,000.[6]

In the short term, layoffs often boost share price performance, and any loss in employee loyalty seems like a smart trade-off. The question is, Are these short-term gains also shortsighted?

Although Wall Street may applaud a layoff, most companies' other stakeholders are not as sanguine. Employees who've been pink-slipped, as well as those who remain (plus their families, communities, and local media), can quickly turn popular sentiment against the offending company, affecting its reputation far into the future. And as we've seen, as the economy shifts and jobs begin to outnumber the people available to fill them, companies will actually have to compete for workers—in some cases, the very ones whom they've let go.

In addition, research shows that mass layoffs can actually *depress* stock prices over time. According to Bain & Co., companies that let go more than 15 percent of their employees during the recession of the early 1990s performed well below average in the three years following the layoffs; results for companies with multiple layoffs were even worse.[7]

Why? Call it the price of losing employee loyalty.

If you haven't thought about quantifying the effect of loyalty, you're not alone. But companies on the leading edge of loyalty know that it has a long-term impact on a wide range of factors, including a company's reputation, productivity, and profitability; customer loyalty and long-term value; brand development; and business growth.

Loyalty and the Bottom Line

"If the person beside you just got shot, you're going to do what you have to do to stay alive, but when the economy turns, you're going to be looking for something else."

—ROBERT MORGAN, PRESIDENT OF THE HUMAN CAPITAL CONSULTING GROUP, SPHERION CORPORATION

In a 2003 MetLife survey, employers said that improving employee retention and increasing employee job satisfaction were among their most important benefits objectives.[8] They may not have made the leap of making employee loyalty a top *business* objective, but these managers are still ahead of the curve, because loyalty is fast becoming the make-or-break factor for business success.

John Miller, senior vice president of sales and marketing for the career management consulting firm Drake Beam Morin, points out that the emotional toll of layoffs translates into measurable losses in productivity. In an interview in *Workforce* magazine, Miller warns that for each employee let go in a layoff, other workers' productivity suffers. Inevitably, employees spend time speculating with colleagues about who's next. Some may simply slow down or slack off—because it doesn't seem that hard work matters any more.[9]

When layoffs affect a disproportionate number of lower and middle managers, there are further consequences. In most organizations, the company "memory" resides in the middle ranks: with those workers who have been with the company for a number of years, have been promoted through the ranks, and have mentored or been mentored by colleagues throughout the organization. The loss or erosion of that institutional memory makes communicating company procedures, culture, and strategies to new or temporary employees more time-consuming, more cumbersome, more prone to error, and as a result, more expensive.

Before companies resort to layoffs, employee benefits become vulnerable. Since typical HR functions, including employee relations, relocation, and training, aren't directly tied to the bottom line, those programs tend to be cut as a first line of defense against falling returns.

Although this strategy may have a positive effect on quarterly P&Ls, it sends a strong signal to employees and potential employees that their growth inside the organization may be limited. When employees feel that their organization isn't committed to their well-being and career development, they're more likely to leave voluntarily for other opportunities.

According to Walker Information's annual report on employee loyalty, just 30 percent of individual employees can be considered "truly loyal" to their current job or employer, and only about half of all workers consider their companies a good place to work.[10] In the retail sector, for instance, which has one of the lowest employee retention rates of any industry, the high turnover rate, according to Bob Kizer, senior vice president of Walker, is a result of "the employer's inability to compensate and train employees."[11]

Sooner or later, of course, recessions end, industries evolve, and company fortunes improve. It's then that companies often realize the opportunity cost of having too few employees ready to do business.

In the early 1990s, telco US West made sweeping cuts in their operations, laying off hundreds of people, from network operations specialists to the people who climb the telephone poles. During the same period, a number of state legislatures lifted company earnings caps, allowing companies such as US West unlimited earnings potential, provided they met specified performance standards. Unfortunately, US West had let go so many workers that it couldn't meet the government's performance specifications, and was fined tens of thousands of dollars. The layoffs also damaged relations with the company's largest unions; a year later, 34,000 workers walked off their jobs in US West's first major strike.

When companies are ready to expand their workforces again, they face a long list of expenses. According to the *MIT Sloan Management Review*, it costs $3,000 just to interview someone—and that's before hiring and training costs kick in. And depending on whom you're hiring and in what capacity, costs for bringing an employee on board and up to speed can be anything from a significant chunk of that employee's salary to an amount that exceeds it by a wide margin. *MIT*'s statistics offer a few examples.[12] On average, it costs:

- From $8,000 to $10,000 to replace a manufacturing employee
- Some $15,000 to replace a retail store clerk
- About 125 percent of first-year compensation to replace an IT worker

Companies that retain their employees over the long run realize that satisfied employees keep hiring and training costs low—because turnover is not a problem.

Can't Loyalty Be Bought?

"Most assuredly, tremendous damage can be done to the morale and commitment of employees any time managers let their self-interest run amok."

—MATT BLOOM, UNIVERSITY OF NOTRE DAME

One trap that some employers fall into is the idea that employee loyalty can be bought. Matt Bloom, associate professor of management at the University of Notre Dame, calls this "mercenary loyalty," a temporary form of loyalty that is easily redirected when another organization is willing to give more. According to Bloom, the mercenary loyalty produced by runaway bonuses, overwhelmingly disproportionate executive salaries, and lifestyle perks is creating an "insidious crisis . . . the demise of true loyalty among many managers and employees in America's companies."[13]

Paula Morrow, a management professor at Iowa State University, sees a similar trend infiltrating the rank and file. In the absence of a culture of loyalty—and with little or no expectation of job security—employees are easily lured to another position by a larger salary, leaving companies vulnerable to a bidding war for top talent. By contrast, Morrow observed in an interview with the *Detroit News* that "companies that can get an emotional form of loyalty from workers get employees who take pride in their products, offer better customer service . . . and [as a result] those companies have less turnover and fewer customer complaints."

Being proud of the product you represent is crucial, but it's only part of a larger picture. In fact, the most loyal employees—and those who offer the best customer service—are not just proud of the products and services they offer, but proud of the companies they work for. Most important, they're proud of themselves and what they're achieving in this world, based on the work they do and the contributions they make to the company's and customers' well-being.

Christine Wright-Isak, Ph.D., president of Northlight Marketing, Inc., a research firm specializing in business sociology, says, "Loyalty is something that comes over and above compensation. The company culture has to consider some intangibles, for instance, the common human need to feel valued."

> *"Corporate leaders I spoke with can't explain why loyalty is important, but they know it affects customer retention. It's a crisis."*
>
> —FREDERICK REICHHELD, AUTHOR OF *LOYALTY RULES*

What makes a customer happy? The product or service has to work, of course, but it's common sense that a good experience shopping or working with your company is going to create the potential for a longer-term relationship. This isn't rocket science, but company leaders tend to forget one crucial element: Customers forge relationships not with the "brand" per se, but with the people they encounter who represent the brand and the products or services it provides.

Reichheld, whose studies focus on customer satisfaction, says that most businesses don't make the logical connection that they need loyal customers in order to grow a profitable business and that they can't have loyal customers without loyal employees.

When Cisco Systems wanted to find out how customers felt about its service, it went right to the source. In-depth and transaction-based customer service surveys helped identify customers' expectations and experiences at a very detailed level. The good news: The collective results showed that Cisco's customers believed in the company's ability to resolve product issues quickly and accurately. The bad news? Customers' actual experience was not always in line with their expectations.

Instead of chastising or punishing its employees for inconsistent performance, Cisco decided to make the employees' jobs more interesting, satisfying, and rewarding.

The company launched an initiative called the Timely Resolution Improvement Project (TRIP), a continuous training and rewards program for the company's technical support engineers, the front line of customer service and satisfaction. TRIP brings the engineers up to standard levels of product knowledge, provides them with communication and customer management skills—and then offers them the chance to continue to improve and upgrade those skill sets. A new performance measurement and reward system offers quarterly bonuses and incentive awards for specific goals, such as time to resolution, customer satisfaction, and the number of cases closed. Everyone in the company is rewarded according to how much customer satisfaction increases.

Cisco's experience is a dramatic example of how more satisfied customers are the result of more motivated employees: In the three quarters immediately following the program's start, customer satisfaction scores improved 50 percent.[14]

Loyal Employees Create Loyal Customers

> *"All that separates you from your competitors are the skills, knowledge, commitment, and abilities of the people who work for you. There is a very compelling business case for this idea: Companies that manage people right will outperform companies that don't by 30 percent to 40 percent."*

> —JEFFREY PFEFFER, STANFORD UNIVERSITY

Honeywell's Global Business Services (GBS) group is one of several high-tech organizations that have realized the critical importance of the employee-customer relationship. Recognizing the inherent limitations of an all-electronic relationship, GBS began to schedule quarterly face-to-face meetings with the senior leaders of client organizations. Together, the GBS team and their clients review current metrics, discuss client issues, and identify any necessary changes in processes and procedures. Once back in their own office, the GBS staff is responsible for making sure that all the relevant people in their organization clearly understand the client's expectations in terms of both service and deliverables.

The quarterly customer feedback sessions, coupled with specific responsibilities and accountability within GBS, ensure that client expectations are regularly met, if not exceeded. And clients respond: Since GBS made the commitment to create more personal contact in employee-customer relationships, customer satisfaction levels have risen 20 percent.

Customers are even willing to pay more for better service. In Walker Information's 2003 study of retail loyalty, sales associate professionalism and fast checkout were cited as two of the top four factors influencing customer loyalty. The report tied service straight to the bottom line, because loyal customers are likely to shop more frequently, spend more on each purchase, and recommend the retailer to others.

It's common sense that if you treat a customer well, that customer will not only return but also pass on information about her pleasant experience to others.[15] When customers begin to sense a lower quality of service, their loyalty begins to be affected—and sales begin to drop.

And as most managers know, this can trigger a vicious cycle. Disaffected consumers are hard to lure back: The cost of acquiring new customers is at least five times the cost of servicing established ones.[16] And when companies find themselves in the trap of continually having to woo back old customers, they have less time, energy, and money available to move the brand—and the business—forward.

How can the cycle be reversed? Most companies want to enjoy the benefits of improved employee loyalty but don't know where to begin. The loyalty factor is available to every company, of any size or type. The roadmap begins on the next page.

PART 2

THE
LOYALTY FACTOR

4

What Is the Loyalty Factor?

"Every business needs loyal employees, loyal customers, and loyal stakeholders. But loyalty . . . requires a management team that treats others with honesty and fairness. And it requires employees and customers to respond in kind. What a simple concept for success: honesty and fairness. Who would have thought?"[1]

—RONALD G. PANTELLO

When it comes to earning employee loyalty, and even customer loyalty, many companies are operating from a deficit of trust. In a Rutgers–University of Connecticut poll, 58 percent of workers surveyed thought that most top executives are interested only in looking out for themselves, even if it harms their company.[2]

As Carl Van Horn, director of the Heldrich Center for Workforce Development at Rutgers University, told the *New York Times,* "American workers are doing very badly. . . . There's high turnover, high instability, a reduction in benefits and a declining loyalty on the part of employers. At the same time, expectations for productivity and quality are going up. It's a bad situation from a worker's standpoint."[3]

Confirming the point, the Conference Board found that job satisfaction has decreased sharply, from 59 percent in 1995 to less than 49 percent in 2003.[4]

Many companies talk about the importance of their employees, but how many of them have instilled that idea into the company culture? How many take the time and effort to find out what employees really want from the job and whether the company needs to make changes—in the organization, technology, processes, or even people—to keep talent from walking out the door?

> *"Employees can, and regularly do, detect false promises and insincerity, especially when the promises get no further than posters on company walls."*[5]
>
> —DOUGLAS K. SMITH

Marketers and business leaders alike often tend to think that loyalty—if it can be achieved at all—is the result of specific, tactical actions, such as employee benefits and perks, ongoing customer communications, or occasional price breaks.

But creating true loyalty is more fundamental, and far less transactional, than these traditional marketing-based approaches suggest.

The Loyalty Factor transcends marketing and its silos of customer acquisition, retention, and winback; it goes far beyond the HR portfolio of hiring practices, payroll, and benefits.

The Loyalty Factor is a comprehensive, integrated vision for managing your organization for greater growth and profitability. The Loyalty Factor is based on a deceptively simple formula, but it's one that we find that many business leaders take for granted— or ignore completely:

Employee loyalty drives customer loyalty, which drives brand loyalty.

With the long-term forecast of jobs outnumbering employees, it is critical for businesses that want to survive to create and maintain a secure foundation of honor, trust, and respect among employees.

No less an observer than *New York Times* columnist William Safire noted that companies have to make loyalty a two-way street. In a prescient column written almost twenty years ago (long before the pension-shattering implosions of Enron and WorldCom), Safire wrote: "Companies have to recognize that employee loyalty is a substantial asset . . . a more loyal work force may not show up in the quarterly earnings, but will help the company survive and prosper."[6]

Loyalty is not something that can be imposed; just like a paycheck, it has to be earned. It is management's job—and its responsibility—to create an atmosphere in which employee loyalty can flourish.

Why Do We Work?

"You can buy a person's hands but you can't buy his heart. His heart is where his enthusiasm, his loyalty is."

—STEPHEN COVEY

An ad campaign for the Principal Financial Group asks, "Why Do We Work?" Increasingly, the answer is not only for a paycheck or benefits, although those are certainly key factors in most people's lives.

Author and management guru Douglas K. Smith says that work is where we find community, meaning, and a sense of purpose.

As a young woman, I remember being offered a new job for substantially more money than the job I had at the time. I called my father, very excited, to tell him the news and get his praise for my achievement. I've never forgotten his words. He said, "The money sounds great. But before you make a decision, try to figure out if you're going to like getting up every morning and going to work at this place."

What makes us want to go to work in the morning? We *have* to go to work if we want to get paid, but we *want* to go to work to exercise our intellectual and creative and physical skills, to use our talents to their best potential. When we have the chance to be part of an organization and contribute to a mission that we believe in and care about, we tend to feel better about ourselves, and about how we're spending the days and hours that we delegate to work. The amount of satisfaction we find in our jobs is critical to that feeling my father described in that long-ago conversation, a feeling that is one of the building blocks of loyalty.

> *"Work is . . . about a search for daily meaning as well as daily bread; for recognition as well as cash; for astonishment rather than torpor."*
>
> —STUDS TERKEL, *WORKING*

The landmark Gallup study "The Twelve Dimensions of a Great Workplace" reported that employees who thought their workplace was "great" were also those who reported receiving recognition and praise for their work, encouragement to develop professionally, and who said that they were treated with respect. Here's a surprise: Participants in the survey did not include financial compensation as one of the twelve most important workplace attributes.[7]

Writing in the *Gallup Management Journal*, Gallup Senior Research Director James K. Harter says, "Most of us crave meaning as well as money through work." Harter goes on to say that emotions physically affect workers' abilities: When they feel that they are making a meaningful contribution, "attention, cognition and performance should increase." On the other hand, employees who feel betrayed, let down, or underutilized can experience an actual loss of memory function, along with a reduced ability "to perform complex tasks."

As Harter says, "The moral is simple: If you satisfy their deep wants, employees become more cognitively and emotionally engaged and will perform better."[8]

In his 1911 book, *Increasing Human Efficiency in Business,* visionary business psychologist and educator Walter Dill Scott wrote about the benefits of cultivating employee loyalty:

> The feeling which workmen entertain for their employer is usually a reflection of his attitude towards them. . . . If he treats his men like machines, looks at them merely as cogs in the mechanism of his affairs, they will function like machines or find other places. . . .
>
> He must identify them with the business, and make them feel that they have a stake in its success and that the organization has an interest in

the welfare of its men. The boss to whom his employees turn in any serious perplexity or private difficulty for advice and aid is pretty apt to receive more than the contract minimum of effort every day and is sure of devoted service in any time of need.[9]

Employee Loyalty Leads to Customer Loyalty

"The change of viewing employees as an asset or a source of revenue production rather than a cost is a whole mind shift for the business community. People are coming to grips with the fact that you make your numbers because of the people you employ."

—JAMES E. COPELAND, JR.,
CHIEF EXECUTIVE OFFICER OF DELOITTE TOUCHE TOHMATSU

Loyalty is like any other good investment: Its returns are compounded over time. Smart leaders recognize that satisfied, smart, motivated employees are a crucial factor in business success.

Research shows that a more satisfied employee is a better team player, shows up for work on time and for more days of work, and, most important, makes more productive use of that time, earning higher performance ratings from his or her employer.

For managers inclined to dismiss loyalty as just a "touchy-feely" piece of management advice, rather than a hard business asset, a 2002 "Controller's Report" in *Business and Management Practices* says, "There is a link between loyalty and corporate performance . . . core accounting measures should begin to look at employee value, not just costs."[10]

Staples CEO Ron Sargent put that idea into practice when he

arrived at the faltering company in 2002. Charged with turning around growth and profitability, Sargent was widely expected to put in austerity measures across the board. Instead, as Sargent explained in an interview with *Business Week,* "I said we're going to squeeze the daylights out of every imaginable cost except two: We are not going to cut back on marketing, and we are not going to cut back on in-store service. In fact, we're spending more in both of those areas."[11]

One of Sargent's first moves was to ask his team to take a fresh look at Staples's customers and their spending patterns. The research showed that owners and managers of small businesses were the heart of Staples's market, responsible for 65 percent of sales and 90 percent of profits. The research also showed that small-business customers wanted more and better in-store service: available, knowledgeable sales reps and fast checkout.[12]

The Staples team now had a focus for its efforts. In order to give its target market the service it needed and wanted, Staples invested in its people, providing intensive training to its sales associates and even increasing the number of sales reps per store. It also changed the product mix, removing hundreds of items targeted toward casual customers and adding more than 600 items suited for small-business owners and managers.[13]

This investment in front-line service people was counterintuitive from a pure cost-cutting standpoint, but it paid off, both in attracting more customers and in producing higher volume per customer. In the first year alone, sales rose 8 percent and the stock price increased significantly.[14] By 2004, only two years after coming on board, Sargent had moved Staples onto the *BusinessWeek* 50, a ranking of America's top-performing companies.

What About the Brand?

"The soft stuff is always harder than the hard stuff."

—ROGER ENRICO

Southwest Airlines famously puts its people first; in fact, half of its short mission statement is about Southwest's commitment to its employees. Southwest has been loyal to that mission statement, and its business model, throughout its thirty-plus-year history: It keeps costs, as well as fares, as low as possible, and it relies on its employees to keep expenses and turnaround time well below those of the competition.

The company's commitment to its vision has earned it a continuing place in the business press, including being named "The Hottest Thing in the Sky" in a 2004 *Fortune* magazine article—not bad for a company with three decades of flying time under its belt.[16]

Speaking at a Boston College Club CEO Luncheon Series in March 2004, Jim Parker, Southwest's former vice chairman and chief executive officer, noted that the company has always responded to the public's demand for great service, an approach that has led directly to thirty-one years of profitability.

Southwest is known to have the highest level of employee satisfaction in the industry. One reason is Southwest's adherence to the Golden Rule: Treat others as you would like to be treated. When Parker was asked by an attendee at the Boston College luncheon whether any employees could explain why they felt so strongly about the company, one employee in the audience called out, "Because the company likes you back."[17]

Southwest's active commitment to its employees has been well documented, but one example will highlight the difference between Southwest and its industry rivals. As we all remember, after the terrorist attacks on the World Trade Center and the Pentagon in September 2001, the nation's passenger flights were grounded for several days, and passenger travel fell off sharply. Once the skies were cleared for passenger flights, Southwest went back to business as usual in every possible way: It didn't cut flights from its normal schedule, and it didn't lay off any workers.[18]

At the same time, as Jackie Huba reports in her book *Creating Customer Evangelists,* a number of Southwest's customers expressed concern over the fate of their favorite airline . . . and the airline staff. Some were so worried that Southwest—like almost all the other airlines—might have to lay off employees that they sent the company letters of support (and in some cases money) to encourage it to retain its workers. Huba begins her book with this excerpt from a letter written in October 2001 by one devoted Southwest customer: "We are encouraging our clients to fly Southwest Airlines. We are buying more stock and we are standing ready to do anything to help. Count on our continuing support."[19]

Over the next two years, the powerful combination of Southwest employees and their customers helped the company continue to be the stock to watch, even in the recession years 2001 and 2002. In 2003, Southwest's earnings, at $442 million, outpaced the earnings of all other U.S. carriers *combined.* Perhaps most significant, in May 2003, Southwest hit another milestone, boarding more domestic customers than any other airline, according to the Department of Transportation.

By way of contrast, rival US Airways cut 14,000 jobs, negotiated $1 billion in annual concessions from workers, and filed for bankruptcy. In April 2003, according to union leaders in Pittsburgh, US Airways's home city, workers at US Airways were "stressed out, angry and frustrated."[20]

Employee Loyalty Drives Customer Loyalty, Which Drives Brand Loyalty

When we look at the three parts of the Loyalty Factor—employee loyalty, which drives customer loyalty, which drives brand loyalty—it's easy to see how all three pieces work together, and often intertwine.

Understanding how each element works independently, however, is key to successfully implementing the Loyalty Factor. So let's take a more in-depth look at each piece of the equation, beginning with part 1 of the Loyalty Factor: employees.

5

Employees, the New Strategic Alliance

"The interests of the Company and its employees are
inseparable."

—WILLIAM COOPER PROCTER,
PROCTER & GAMBLE, 1919

Americans, more than almost any other people on earth, like
to work, taking pride in what they do and in what they
achieve both emotionally and financially. According to the U.S.
Bureau of Labor Statistics, more of the U.S. working-age population is employed than that of any other nation except the Nether-
lands—including Japan, Korea, Germany, France, and the U.K.[1]

The average American still works thirty-five hours a week—
the same as workers in Japan, but more than the average European.
An average workweek in France is twenty-nine hours; in the U.K.
thirty-three hours; and in Germany, twenty-eight hours.

Even so, research indicates that employees don't think their companies care about them: Sixty percent of respondents to one survey said that employers showed less concern for employees than they did for the "financial bottom line," and a similar proportion felt that employers did not demonstrate enough loyalty to long-term employees.[2]

And yet, whether they're inventing and designing robotics, finishing a component on a manufacturing assembly line, planning a site location, or greeting a person who walks into a store, employees are the lifeblood of every business, in every industry . . . your most fundamental, critical link to your customers and prospects, and the single most valuable asset in your organization.

Developing the New Employee Alliance

"It is not my intention to do away with government. It is rather to make it work—work with us, not over us; stand by our side, not ride on our back. Government can and must provide opportunity, not smother it; foster productivity, not stifle it."

—RONALD W. REAGAN, FIRST INAUGURAL ADDRESS, JANUARY 20, 1981

The late President Reagan said it well: The role of our institutions is to provide opportunity. For business, that includes creating opportunities for employees at every level of the organization, a strategy that guarantees a higher degree of company loyalty. This, in turn, requires managers to view employees as valuable partners, rather than mere cost centers that drain investment capital through salary, benefits, and overhead. Employees—always an organization's secret weapon—are without question the single most important asset to cultivate in the years to come.

Virtually all company leaders are engaged daily in the business of creating strategic alliances, with the goal of increasing market share and competitive strength. Classically, these alliances are with partner companies, capital investors, and even local governments. In the context of the Loyalty Factor, however, employee relationships are also critical long-term strategic partnerships.

What does it mean to treat employees as strategic partners? At ConocoPhillips Canada, for instance, Judy Walton, human resources vice president, told a seminar audience that it meant "engaging the entire organization to achieve particular performance targets and elevating the capabilities of all employees."[3]

Ricardo Semler, CEO of Semco SA, went one better: He literally made every one of his employees a strategic partner, with an emotional and a financial stake in the company's success.

In Search of the Dispensable CEO

"I've heard many managers refer to their employees as their best asset. While this is a positive step in the right direction, employees mean even more to a business. Employees represent a company's greatest group of investors. Employees invest their personal time, energy, attention and dedication to a company's mission. And like investors, employees have a lot of organizations and companies to choose from."[4]

—MEL KLEIMAN, MANAGING PARTNER, THE HIRE TOUGH GROUP

As a young CEO, Ricardo Semler followed familiar guidelines to revive his father's ailing ship-parts manufacturing company. Only twenty-one when he took the company helm, he slashed the workforce, acquired new companies, courted capital partners, and micromanaged as many details as he could in a workday that averaged more than sixteen hours.

Semler's hard-charging, nonstop schedule wound up having an unexpected effect. When he was still only in his twenties, Semler collapsed during a factory tour; after a checkup, a local doctor provided a second tour, leading Semler through the elegant cardiac wing of the local hospital. Semler made the kind of decision he was best known for: impulsive, ambitious, and crystal clear. In order to avoid an early death, he would change his lifestyle; to do so, he had to reinvent his company.

Semler's goal, he says, was to become "dispensable." Instead of micromanaging, Semler decided to create a workplace democracy, characterized by freedom, independence, and personal responsibility on the part of every employee.

That decision led to some unusual strategies.

Semler combed through his company's infrastructure, eliminating all traces of what he called "corporate oppression," from time clocks and dress codes to organization charts and private offices.

Semler has written two books describing in detail his experience transforming Semco, but the core of his strategy was to empower employees—every single employee, up and down the line—to make their own decisions. Semco employees set their own hours and even their own salaries; hire and, if necessary, fire their colleagues; and purchase everything they need, from laptop computers to sixteen-wheeler trucks to office supplies.

Semler also set up a profit-sharing system, motivating employees to find savings and efficiencies in every aspect of their operation—including staffing. All employees have access to the company financials, so that they can gauge their success and compare their results with those of other departments.

"We always assume that we're dealing with responsible adults, which we are," Semler told an interviewer. "When you start treating employees like adolescents . . . that's when you start to bring out the adolescent in people."

The more freedom Semler gave his staff to manage their own jobs and organizations, the more versatile, productive, and loyal they became, and the better Semco performed. Between 1998 and 2004, Semco's revenues grew more than 600 percent, from $35 million to $212 million; the workforce increased from several hundred to three thousand. Employee turnover was a virtually unheard-of one percent.

Semler's story is compelling, although, as he admits, the process of transforming his company was hardly seamless and wouldn't necessarily work for a publicly held firm.[5,6,7]

Has Semler met his goal of becoming dispensable? Perhaps: He felt comfortable enough to spend the summer of 2004 away from his desk, as a guest lecturer at the Harvard Business School.

How many CEOs have that kind of confidence in their employees' ability to manage the store?

Cultivating Loyal Employees

"The fields of industry are strewn with the bones of those organizations whose leadership . . . didn't realize that the only assets that could not be replaced easily were the human ones."

—LE ROY H. KURTZ, GENERAL MOTORS

Ricardo Semler's successful strategy may be too extreme for most of us—after all, I don't know too many CEOs who actually want to become dispensable!

The basic message, though, is clear: What employees crave is a relationship with a supervisor, and a team, who they can trust and who places trust in them. They are looking for colleagues who will listen to them, treat them fairly, and value their contributions to the company.

The old tools for rewarding employees—competitive wages, benefits, and incentives—are still important. But more than ever, they are just the price of entry for hiring or retaining the employees you value. If your company relies solely on a compensation and benefits package to attract and retain loyalty, over time there's a good likelihood that you'll be caught in a price war for the talent you want. When your only leverage is financial, you can either choose to outbid your competitor or let a good employee choose another home.

Industry experts already estimate that two-thirds of all employee departures are voluntary.[8] If that is true for your company, you have an opportunity—in fact, an obligation—to institute the changes needed to create the Loyalty Factor.

> *"Today loyalty is the only thing that matters. But it isn't blind loyalty to the company. It's loyalty to your colleagues, loyalty to your team, loyalty to your project, loyalty to your customers . . . and loyalty to yourself."*[9]
>
> —TOM PETERS

The authors of the Gallup study "First Break All the Rules," which analyzed interviews with one million employees and eighty thousand managers, summed up the results firmly and concisely: "People leave managers, not companies. If you have a turnover problem, look first to your managers."

Sprint PCS experienced that dynamic firsthand. According to consultant Craig R. Taylor, a new Web-based exit interview revealed that over two-thirds of Sprint's departing employees would have been open to staying, if only their management had done something to keep them.

At every level of the company, each employee's relationship with his or her manager provides the clearest picture of that employee's value to the company. The managers who are most effective at cultivating loyalty are "player-coaches"—those who take an active, measurable role in the business, while providing encouragement, training, and support for their direct reports.

Eastern Bank, the largest independent, mutually owned commercial bank in New England, created a companywide system of recognition and rewards, and empowered its managers and supervisors to make it work.

When a manager sees or hears of an employee providing exemplary service, he can give that individual an award right on the spot. The employee can even choose the award; it might be a gift certificate or an Eastern Bank premium item. Every quarter, employees are asked to nominate a colleague on any level, from manager to vice president to secretary, for an "Above and Beyond" award. All of the annual winners are honored at Eastern's annual Quality Awards Dinner. Eastern even encourages its employees to send thank-you notes to one another for a job well done.

Eastern's assets grew from $180 million in 1976 to more than $4.6 billion by 2004.[10] Stanley Lukowski, chairman and CEO of Eastern Bank, gives credit for the bank's success to a combination of the company's vision for growth and the people who make it happen. As he told us, "Success is built on clearly determining where you want to go and who will get you there. The who in this case is all encompassing: It is the employees, it is the customers, it is the vendors, it is every single person that Eastern Bank comes in contact with. It is ensuring that every one of these individuals understands the common purpose and is motivated to achieve it."

Dell: Creating a Winning Culture

"When [Thomas Jefferson] lived in Europe, [he] wanted to create an aristocracy of virtues and talent in the United States. That is our company [mission]."[11]

—KEVIN ROLLINS, PRESIDENT & COO, DELL

Back in the late 1990s, when it seemed like technology companies could never stumble, cultivating employee loyalty was a nonissue: People were drawn to high-tech companies for the promise of quick wealth and early retirement.

Michael Dell's story, of course, is one of the classic tales of the New Economy. Dell founded his company in 1984 with $1,000 and a new idea—to bypass the retailer and sell computer systems directly to customers. As the business took off, Dell's direct-to-customer business model demanded a trained, motivated workforce. In a blazing economy, employee success was defined by beating ever-more-aggressive business goals. The market, the economy, and the business model combined to create 300 to 400 percent growth year after year.

Employee retention was a simple matter of numbers: Top producers were able to stay; others were at risk. In an interview with *Newsweek*, President and COO Kevin Rollins described the prerecession management style as "kick fannies, take names." Managers were expected to meet tough goals, and those expectations were constantly revised—always in an upward direction. Failure was simply not tolerated.[12]

Dell's unforgiving performance measures were tempered by the promise of juicy financial rewards. At the time, stock options (the incentive of choice) represented tantalizing future assets. For those with unrealized options at the turn of the century, however, their imagined wealth—the reward envisioned for the no-holds-barred work ethic that permeated Dell's Round Rock headquarters—stayed imaginary.

Between August 2000 and January 2001, as the entire technology market began to stumble, Dell's stock lost half its value.[13]

Employee morale fell in lockstep with the stock price. Options with higher strike prices became worthless, and the single most important reason for all that hard work—and commitment to the company—vanished.[14] Two rounds of layoffs (the first in the company's fifteen-year history) did nothing to help morale; company research found that nearly half of all employees would make even a lateral move to another company, given the opportunity.

The problem was new and perplexing: How could Dell keep its best employees without the promise (and, as we've seen, it was, after all, just a promise) of big payoffs? Dell realized that the carrot-and-stick management strategy that had worked so well during the boom years had to go if it wanted to keep its best employees and weather the downturn.

Paul McKinnon, Dell's senior vice president for human resources, described the company's next step as a "self-discovery process." For the first time, the company's executive team looked beyond the business model to understand what would make Dell a company that could survive in the long term.

Just as Dell had used relentless analysis of the numbers to motivate employees during the boom years, it turned a methodical eye on what Rollins initially called the "corporate foo-foo."

Following the model of their rigorous sales and revenue reviews, leaders were called upon to examine their professional strengths and weaknesses—in public, in front of their employees.

Michael Dell himself kicked things off with a highly personal, painful assessment of his own flaws as a manager and leader. Dell's first audience was his direct reports, but he was not content to leave the example he set behind closed doors: He had the entire speech videotaped and shown to every manager in the company.[15]

Clearly, Dell Inc. was no longer a company where performance would be based solely on the numbers. With Michael Dell putting himself first in line, managers were on notice that human skills—listening, responding, leadership—were a crucial part of their job descriptions.

"If you look at the typical corporation, the book value of its hard assets is a third or less of its market value. The

rest of the value gets on the elevator and goes home at the end of the day."

—PROFESSOR LYNN A. STOUT, UCLA

In order to measure managers' performance, the company created a twice yearly employee survey called "Tell Dell." Employees were asked to respond to about thirty statements; the answers to five of these statements provide the core metrics used to calculate results, including progress from the previous survey.[16]

The poll was Dell's signal to its employees that a culture shift was under way: Employees would be the ones to say whether Dell was becoming a better place to work and whether their managers seemed to care about their staff at least as much as they cared about the bottom line. Every vice president, every director, and certain department managers were expected to improve their results 20 percent from the previous survey, and raises and bonuses were tied to those results.

In a fundamental way, the corporate culture remained the same, despite the shift in perspective: Employees responded to the mandate for soul-searching as readily as they'd responded to demands for increased sales during the go-go years. The company's initial survey got a 90 percent response rate, and by the time the second survey was fielded, scores had in fact improved 20 percent in virtually every part of the company.

Dell didn't leave its leaders to work in a vacuum. In order to help managers continue to improve their skills and create an active dialogue with employees, Dell instituted an annual series of leadership meetings. The program is explicitly about Dell's expectations and performance standards.

The program is also designed to strengthen communication within departmental teams. It starts with a daylong seminar for senior management run by Michael Dell and Kevin Rollins; each manager in turn leads the same program for his or her direct reports until the information has been shared throughout the company.

The program doesn't let managers hide behind a presentation. From Michael Dell and Kevin Rollins on down, company managers share their scores from the Tell Dell survey; the goal for each manager is to eventually reach—and maintain—a 75 percent approval rate. Far from being a one-way conversation, the meetings are also an opportunity for employees to discuss their expectations and make suggestions for improvement in their boss's performance over the next six months.

The new emphasis on open communication and measurable results in management behavior is only one part of Dell's post-boom strategy. After sixteen years in business, the company created what Paul McKinnon calls "a statement of our aspirations as a company." Developed by senior management in Round Rock, the one-page statement was circulated to Dell's vice presidents around the world for discussion before it was shared with the rank and file.

As a redefinition of the company's goals and identity, the name of this new mission statement is revealing. Called "The Soul of Dell," it has five components: the Dell team, customers, direct relationships, global citizenship, and winning. The complete statement appears on Dell's Web site.[17]

Employees reacted skeptically to this new characterization: Soft and quasi-religious, it did not seem representative of the company that they worked for, and the change, while potentially welcome, was unexpected. Here again, management provided multiple opportunities for internal conversation and discussion. In meetings that ranged from town-hall-style presentations to brown-bag lunches, employees were given a forum to talk about the company's new direction, express their opinions, and ask questions in a give-and-take environment.

Dell didn't lose its financial aspirations, or its drive to increase sales. In 2002, after creating its new, friendlier management policies, Dell revived its tradition of setting newsworthy goals. This time, it announced a drive to double annual sales to $60 billion by 2006.[18]

Bolstered by a management that honors their contributions and cultivates their loyalty, Dell employees once again rose to the challenge. By year-end 2003, Tell Dell results showed that 57 percent of employees would stay at Dell if they were offered a similar position elsewhere, up six points from the previous survey and the mirror image of the results only two years before, when a similar percentage had said that they would leave at the first opportunity.

And for any remaining skeptics who haven't yet come to believe that employee loyalty has a measurable effect on business results, there's one last note: As of early 2004, Dell stock was up 24 percent versus its previous two years, when Tell Dell, and the culture that surrounds it, was just getting started.

Building on the Foundation of Employee Loyalty

Why is employee loyalty so important? As we discussed in Chapter 2, by 2011, available jobs are expected to outnumber available workers by 4.3 million, and by 2031 there could be as many as 35 million jobs lacking qualified workers. Those numbers alone underscore the importance of developing the Loyalty Factor in your organization.

Creating, nourishing, and cherishing employee loyalty is the bedrock of the Loyalty Factor. And as we'll see, it provides a solid foundation for the second key element of the Loyalty Factor: creating customer loyalty.

6

Loyal Employees Are Your Number One Marketing Tool

"What makes the difference, what distinguishes one company from another, is its relationship with the customer."[1]

—ROSANNE D'AUSILIO, PH.D., PRESIDENT,
HUMAN TECHNOLOGIES GLOBAL, INC.

Customer satisfaction, customer loyalty, customer centricity, customer care. Does your organization use any of these terms? We hear and use these buzzwords so often that it's easy to forget what they mean: Loyal customers are what keep us in business.

But as much as we talk about making customers happy, the

average U.S. company doesn't pay a lot of real attention to the people who purchase its products or services. When you consider that the average U.S. company loses half its customers every five years, it's easy to see that many companies haven't paid enough attention, or the right kind of attention, to keeping their customers loyal, year after year.[2]

This is an expensive proposition: A Purdue study confirms that acquiring a new customer costs 500 percent more than keeping a current customer. Other studies suggest that customer acquisition can be up to ten times more costly than retention. And these figures don't take into account a loyal customer's lifetime value, that is, the profit that customer generates with every transaction she makes with your company.

So perhaps it's no surprise that a Gallup Poll concluded, "Today, the search for the ties that bind customers to brands has taken on fresh urgency." Or that, as *New York Times* advertising columnist Stuart Elliot reported, advertising and marketing executives are "frantically searching for ways to forge more emotional connections with fractious, and fractionated, consumers that differ from conventional methods like running 30-second television commercials and print advertisements."[3]

What Does Your Customer *Really* Want?

"Quality in a service or product is not what you put into it. It is what the client or customer gets out of it."
—PETER DRUCKER

The answer to that frantic search is closer to home than those executives may suspect.

When the Forum Corporation asked consumers to rank the importance of various factors in creating a "good customer experience," advertising and promotion ranked only 2.8 on a seven-point scale. In contrast, "actions taken in response to a problem or request" ranked 6.33 and "the employee who served the person" ranked 6.24. Over 60 percent of the people surveyed had switched brand loyalties at some point—not because of product defects or other tangible issues, but because of poor service and lack of personal attention.

As author and consultant Chuck Martin, chairman and CEO of NFI Research, describes, while "the overwhelming majority of executives and managers *say* their organizations are customer-driven, and that customer service is at the top of the list . . . tactics throughout the ranks do not always align with pronouncements at the top."

As we'll see, stand-out companies find that the differentiating factor in building customer loyalty and long-term profitability is something that every company talks about but not every employee is educated to do: provide exceptional customer service.

Building a Loyal Future

"You have got to be out there to be able to meet customers' needs, one transaction at a time."

—ROBERT A. NIBLOCK, PRESIDENT, LOWE'S COMPANIES

Why did the home improvement industry have to examine its customer service strategy? It's a matter of demographics: It seemed that one day men made all the buying decisions about drywall, tools, paint, and hardware, and the next day the stores were full of women. That change didn't happen overnight, of course, but the trends are startling: According to the National Association of Realtors, single women are the fastest-growing segment of home buyers, including those buying condominiums and second homes.

Fannie Mae estimates that by the year 2010, there will be 31 million U.S. households headed by women—nearly a third of total U.S. households.[4]

When Lowe's stores fielded its own research, it discovered that women initiate 80 percent of all home improvement projects, regardless of whether they're married or single, and 94 percent of all female home owners have completed a home improvement project on their own at least once.[5]

Similarly, Home Depot found that 80 percent of the women it surveyed were planning at least one home improvement project, ranging from painting or wallpapering, to replacing doors, windows, or ceiling fixtures, to landscaping their yards or gardens.

How did each company handle the challenge of serving the changing market?

Lowe's began an aggressive strategy to court more women and to build sales from its current female customers, while not alienating the other (male) half of its consumer base. Lowe's saw its female customers as being segmented into two main categories: "serial renovators" (home owners who are continually upgrading their kitchens, baths, and other rooms) and "home entertainers," described by Lowe's President Robert A. Niblock as "primarily younger, educated professional women who are brand loyal."[6]

One of the first things the company changed was the stores themselves. Lighting, flooring, and other products that were high on women's shopping lists were moved to more visible areas, the aisles were widened to give customers more personal space as they shopped, and shelves were reorganized to make popular products easier to reach.[7]

In a more dramatic departure from the typical retail store, Lowe's also created a full-time, professional workforce in its retail locations. It's a more costly strategy than employing as many part-timers as possible; the benefits, however, are even more valuable. Lowe's found that turnover went down, retention improved, and customers had increased access to a more knowledgeable, service-oriented staff.[8]

At the company's 2004 annual meeting, Lowe's chairman and CEO, Robert L. Tillman, recognized the contributions of all 150,000 employees to the company's "record performance in 2003," a performance that included a 48 percent increase in the company's stock price in 2003 and a 22 percent increase in 2004 first-quarter sales. The changes that Lowe's implemented earned it the #50 spot on the 2004 Fortune 500; the company was also named one of *Fortune*'s Most Admired Specialty Retailers.

And Home Depot? With its sales growth running behind Lowe's, it is spending heavily to modernize its stores and train its employees to regain the edge that the company once had in exceptional customer service. As at Lowe's, the push is coming from the top: CEO and GE veteran Bob Nardelli is taking the challenge seriously, making customer service a priority for all 300,000 employees.[9]

In 2003, Home Depot launched a popular series of workshops geared toward helping women learn to do their own remodeling projects. The company reported that between 2003 and 2004, 200,000 women had attended a "Do-It-Herself" workshop.

When Nardelli came on board in December 2000, one of his signature moves was to visit as many stores as possible, checking out the product mix, store environment, and staff knowledge and attitudes, and talking to the people who know more than almost anyone about what makes the company tick: its front-line employees. He even cases out the competition, making personal visits to Lowe's to see firsthand what his rival is doing for its customers.[10,11]

Bob Nardelli and Robert L. Tillman may be approaching their customers differently, but they're both starting where it counts: with their own employees. Lowe's has been reaping the rewards of its early start, but given Bob Nardelli's track record, we don't expect Home Depot to stay behind for long.

The Business Value of Belief

"You gotta believe."

— TUG MCGRAW, 1973 NEW YORK METS

How does a Lowe's or a Home Depot convince any customer that its store is the best for her needs? I've yet to meet a CEO who doesn't believe that his product isn't "the best," but how is that vision communicated most effectively to customers?

In their book, *Selling Yourself to Others*, Kevin Hogan and William Horton write that "the 21st Century Selling Model" includes not only understanding the beliefs, values, attitudes, and lifestyles of the customer (something that is second nature to most marketers) but understanding those of the salesperson as well.[12]

Why are employee beliefs important? Because in order to communicate your company's message most effectively, everyone in your organization, from salespeople to cashiers, has to believe in what she's doing. This is true even of the people who aren't in classic customer-facing positions—those in marketing, operations, or even finance—because in order to do their jobs well, they need to "sell" their ideas and needs up and down the chain of command.

Belief is one of the most motivating, most persuasive tools we have. Unfortunately, it can't be forced; it has to be nurtured and developed, first by an understanding of employees' and customers' current beliefs, and then by determining the information that will help reshape negative or even neutral beliefs into positive ones.

Why do customers make the choices they do? Customers come to your company because they hope to find a product or service that they need—even if sometimes they don't know what they need until they find it. That belief—that your company can fulfill these spoken or unspoken needs—is often directly related to the attitudes and beliefs of your employees. A knowledgeable, enthusiastic employee can often turn even a skeptic into a satisfied customer, one who has the potential not only to continue spending money with your company but to refer friends and colleagues who will do the same.

So what do employees need to believe? According to management guru Doug Smith, they have to feel that they're contributing to a worthy goal, and that the organization shares their values. Loyalty Factor's own research shows that effective, enthusiastic employees tend to have three key beliefs:

1. I believe in myself and my ability to do my job well.
2. I believe in the company I represent: the quality of its leadership and goals, and that it treats people fairly and recognizes that employees are part of its ability to succeed.
3. I believe in the quality of the products and services I'm selling/developing/supporting.

If those three beliefs exist, the power of those convictions radiates from each employee to the customers that employee serves.[13]

One of our clients, a pharmaceutical company, asked us to help it market its diabetes supplies. The competition in the disposable needle market was eating our client alive, and it decided that it could develop a critical edge by training its customer service reps to sell the product more effectively. The reps knew all the technical specs, the pricing, delivery times, and so on, but something was clearly missing in their presentation to potential customers.

When we went out to talk to the reps, we found that there was good news and bad news. The good news was that very few of the reps had diabetes. The bad news was that, as a result, virtually none of them had any experience using the product, and so the information that they gave customers was only what they had learned from reading company marketing brochures. They certainly understood the product, but they had no reason to believe in it—and that lack of emotional connection made their sales technique less effective.

So what did we do? It was simple: We opened a case of the product and asked each rep to prick himself with one of the needles he was selling. It took a little convincing, but to their surprise, the reps found that, just as the product literature said, the needles didn't hurt. Once they knew that, it was amazing what they were able to do with the information, and with the belief in their product that only firsthand experience can bring.

A Texas-Sized Attitude Adjustment

"In the dictionary, under 'fanatic,' it says 'overly zealous or obsessed with.' "[14]

—DAVID BRYCE, VICE PRESIDENT, CUSTOMER CARE, RACKSPACE

When employees believe in their mission, their products, and their ability to succeed in the job, you've turned them into fans of the company and the product. According to my dictionary, "fan" is derived from a stronger word: fanatic.

Jump onto Rackspace's Web site, and it pops out at you immediately: a little pink figure, arms stretched overhead, holding a black box. Next to it are the words "Fanatical Support™ makes the difference."[15]

San Antonio–based Rackspace is a Web-hosting company that decided that its future depended on outstanding customer service. Founded in 1998, Rackspace is now one of the fastest-growing managed hosting companies in the world. Its approach, the company says, is simple: combining "extensive expertise in managed hosting and stay[ing] focused on our customer." And what does it mean to offer Fanatical Support? According to the company Web site, "It is what guides us to go above and beyond our customers' expectations when managing mission-critical hosting environments . . . [offering] proactive service . . . based on the unique needs of each individual customer."

High-tech consulting firm Frost & Sullivan awarded Rackspace its 2002 and 2003 Customer Value Enhancement awards for the way the company "has raised the bar of service for its segment and enhanced the value of its service to new and existing customers."[16]

The timing of those awards is no accident. By its own admission, between its founding and the crash of 2001, Rackspace was a typically arrogant dot-com company. In a 2004 interview with *Fast Company*, customer care vice president David Bryce was not shy about revealing that "the tech-support staff appeared to feel no urgency about addressing problems . . . and sometimes seemed openly hostile to customers."[17]

That might have been acceptable in the go-go years, when revenue was piling up like manna from heaven. When the crash came, though, CEO Graham Weston reorganized the company so that its focus would be on the people who bring in the revenue: customers.

This couldn't happen without the active support of—and a changed attitude on the part of—employees.

Weston redeployed his staff, automating critical workflow and putting more employees to work directly with customers. He demonstrated the importance of customer care by providing each customer with the direct cell phone numbers of senior management, including himself. Every customer-facing employee was provided with additional training to improve her customer service skills, as well as to upgrade her technology knowledge.

Some of the new rules for customer service might have been second nature to an earlier generation of employees, but they set a new bar for the young Rackspace team (a/k/a the "Rackers"). The first rule? Any Racker who criticized a customer could lose his job.

There were a number of other items on the list of new expectations for employee behavior, including communicating with customers more frequently, finding ways to exceed customer expectations before being asked, and making it easy (and pleasant) for people to work with Rackspace.

If the Rackers were shaken up a little by the new rules, those weren't the end of the changes that management put in place. Rackspace physically moved many of its people out of their departments, setting them up in customer-focused teams that included account managers, tech specialists, and even a member of the billing department. Every team was dedicated to specific customers, and every customer call was fielded by a team member.

Team members work in shifts around the clock, so that if a Web site goes down at 3 A.M., someone from Rackspace is there to fix it. They call customers every month to review usage and performance statistics, opening the door to a change in service plans if the customer sees the need.

Working across a desk from each other on a daily basis, talking face-to-face instead of via phone or e-mail, and having a common purpose strengthens the bonds between employees and has allowed each team to form deeper, multifaceted relationships with customers. Rackspace monitors customer satisfaction on a daily basis: The more satisfied the customer, the more employees are rewarded; apart from the emotional rewards, each employee's compensation is directly tied to team performance, both financially and in terms of customer satisfaction.

The results? In 2004, Rackspace announced that 2003 revenues had grown 48 percent over 2002 (almost five times the industry average) and pretax profits were up 134 percent.[18]

Not every company can (or should) make such dramatic changes so quickly. Big-box retailer Best Buy, for instance, realized it too had to step up service in a changing industry, in this case, discount electronics stores. For Best Buy, it wasn't a question of adjusting employee attitudes, but of adjusting its strategy to address a new kind of customer need.

Best Buy started small, and smart, to see what would happen once it created a service-based culture in a price-based industry.

Managing Risk, and Reaping Rewards

"We encouraged our store associates to create better relationships with customers. They brought passion, energy, and creativity to this initiative, and they are the primary reason our test was successful."[19]

—MIKE KESKEY, PRESIDENT, U.S. BEST BUY STORES

It's 3 A.M., and your computer is behaving badly. Can you fix it? No. And how do you know that your computer is misbehaving in the middle of the night? Because you're working on a presentation, or speech, or report due at the start of business the next day.

If you bought your computer at retailer Best Buy, you can call the company (yes, at 3 A.M.), and its promise to you is that one of its employees will show up at your door to fix the problem. When you open the door, you'll see someone in an outfit straight out of *The Blues Brothers*: white shirt, black tie, white socks, black shoes, badges, and sunglasses. You've just met the Geek Squad.

If you look out to the street, you might even see the squad's signature car parked at the curb: the Geekmobile, a black-and-white VW Beetle sporting the company logo.[20,21]

At Best Buy, management realized that the company had to differentiate its retail stores from other price-based electronics outlets. It knew that the company's customers wanted more when it came to owning, operating, and fixing the technology they bought, and its unique solution was an old-fashioned one: customer service.

If you need a house call, Best Buy's Geek Squad is available by appointment, or even for emergencies. Geek Squad service is also available in Best Buy stores, trading at-home convenience for a lower service price.

Even so, consumers are willing to pay for the convenience of house calls for jobs ranging from installing new software to figuring out why the screen just went blank. The added convenience doesn't come cheaply: Price tags of $200 or more are common for anything more than garden-variety tasks.[22]

How does the Geek Squad fit into Best Buy's larger vision? It's part of Best Buy's new strategy of "customer centricity," a model for empowering employees to deal directly with customer needs. As Best Buy vice chairman and CEO Brad Anderson explained, "Our customer centricity initiative enables us to engage more deeply with customers by empowering our employees to deliver tailored products, solutions and services to customers."

Best Buy's experiment with the Geek Squad started in test markets before being rolled out across the country. The company used the same formula when it moved into its next phase: making the classic retail stores more customer friendly.[23]

In 2003, the company selected thirty-two stores to serve as "labs"; the group included both underachievers and high-performing stores, all measured against a panel of control stores. Company designers changed the look of the test stores from the price-based, warehouse feeling of a typical Best Buy to a somewhat more upscale, lifestyle-oriented atmosphere, with product information that showed how products fit into customers' lives and less emphasis on price or technical specs.

Most significantly, Best Buy placed a new focus on its sales associates. Instead of hiring staffers who could simply help customers locate products and run checkout, the company reached out to find more sales-oriented professionals who would understand and deliver the new customer-friendly strategy.

Each of these new hires receives thirty days of training, which one reporter likened to studying at "some fast-track MBA academy." The training introduces the new associates to Best Buy's five target customer segments (see the list given here), the experience each group wants in the store, and how the members of each group interact at home with their new purchase.[24]

Best Buy's Best Bets

Best Buy's first test of its customer-centric strategy targeted five customer groups, all selected for their growth potential. Sales associates learn how to match products and service with each specific customer.

- The affluent professional who wants the best technology and demands excellent service
- The active younger male who wants the latest technology and entertainment
- The family man who wants technology that improves his life
- The busy suburban mom who wants to enrich her children's lives
- The small-business customer

Source: Best Buy.

Each new "customer-centric" store has 15 percent more sales associates than a standard Best Buy location, giving each customer the opportunity to work with one associate from the first product question to the at-home installation of a new purchase. Some associates are specially trained in assisting customers in the particular demographic groups that Best Buy has targeted for growth, such as well-to-do "soccer moms."

Every customer gets at least one follow-up call after the sale to make sure that everything is working as promised. This relationship opens the door to suggesting more products—increasing the potential for both higher volume and longer relationships with each customer.

According to U.S. Best Buy stores president Mike Keskey, "Our employees are energized because they have both the responsibility and the accountability to make decisions and drive innovation based on their knowledge of the customer. They behave like owner/operators and really understand the customer and financial impact of their decisions."

Every morning, sales associates and managers in the customer-centric stores meet before the doors open to customers, reviewing performance numbers from the day before. With the information from these meetings, associates are given the freedom to make decisions that will be better for both the customers and Best Buy's bottom line, including inventory selection and product placement.

How did customers respond to the new concept? The numbers tell the story.

At an analysts' meeting in the spring of 2004, Best Buy's executive VP of finance and chief financial officer, Darren Jackson, provided the following results for the customer-centric "lab" experiment. In the previous quarter, traditional Best Buy stores' sales had increased 10 percent, compared with 17 percent in the customer-centric stores, the average transaction was $100 versus $104, and the sales close rate was 51 percent versus 57 percent.

The concept was a go: Best Buy plans to roll out its customer-centric concept to more stores in the coming months.

Customer Loyalty Leads to Brand Loyalty

So what do these stories show? Each one underscores the power of an enthusiastic, motivated sales force to energize customers and deliver increased sales. If you wanted, you could stop right there and still improve company morale, productivity, and bottom-line results.

But why stop now? The third element of the Loyalty Factor is the peak experience that most companies aim for and not many achieve: becoming a brand that customers love and can't live without.

The Loyalty Factor
and the Brand

"Brands speak to two people, the consumer and the
employee."

—BRIAN COLLINS, EXECUTIVE CREATIVE DIRECTOR,
OGILVY AND MATHER

A loyal customer hasn't just picked a product—she's made a lifestyle choice. Your company is a fundamental part of that customer's existence, whether it's the Bose stereo she can't imagine living without, the household cleaner that beats all others, or the car that precisely fits her personality.

Jackie Huba, author of *Creating Customer Evangelists*, says that the highest form of loyalty is not repeat purchase, but "when a customer will put his or her reputation on the line and tell someone else, 'you have got to buy this product. You have got to engage this company.'"[1]

Good customers create good WOM—good word of mouth. Up to one in four customers may actively recommend (or actively not recommend) your company, based on the experiences they've had with your product or service. Some sources say that word of mouth is increasingly becoming a consumer's first (and most predominant) form of information.

Tom Peters found that, on average, a customer who has had a poor experience with a company will tell nine to ten people. Some unhappy customers will really spread the bad word: Peters found that 13 percent of dissatisfied consumers will tell *twenty or more* of their closest friends and associates—or possibly anybody else who'll listen.

> *"If you make customers unhappy in the physical world, they might each tell six friends. If you make customers unhappy on the Internet, they can each tell 6,000 friends."*
>
> —JEFF BEZOS

What do American Express, Harley-Davidson, Waterford, Ben & Jerry's, and Victoria's Secret have in common? They're all companies that sell more than products—they are part of a lifestyle with which customers can identify. Over time, these companies have created a synergistic relationship with their customers, so that the experiences customers have with the product, as well as with the retail stores carrying it, customer service, billing, catalogs, and every other touch point, reinforce their belief in the brand and its ability to change, improve, or maintain their quality of life.

KitchenAid, for example, sells mixers, blenders, and other small and major appliances. Take a moment sometime and look at its Web site. Right on the home page, there's a link to "KitchenAid Conversation," an online bulletin board where KitchenAid users are invited to share their experiences, questions, and recipes. One of the dozens of forums is called "Inspiring KitchenAid Experiences." Hundreds of people have logged on to read about customers' KitchenAid memories—some of which include generations of loyal users within a single family.

Customer "Jenny P." even asked how she could find paint for her kitchen walls that would match the color of her KitchenAid mixer. After complimenting her enthusiasm, service rep "kitchenaidkelly01" told Jenny how to match the KitchenAid color at a paint or hardware store.[2]

Unhappy customers aren't ignored: Defective products are replaced for free within the first year of purchase, and the company has even been known to replace a product long after the warranty has expired.[3]

KitchenAid is a brand that Saatchi & Saatchi CEO Kevin Roberts would call a "lovemark." Roberts, author of *Lovemarks: The Future Beyond Brands,* understands the power of customers' passion in evolving a brand from something they use to something they'd rather not live without.[4]

Creating a lovemark, Roberts says, begins with the simplest of strategies: listening to the customer. Hearing customers' stories about how they use the product and what their experiences have been over time will give you all the information you need to create the experiences they want to have—whether that leads to introducing new technologies into your back-end office systems or rewarding employees who best exemplify your brand and its values.

Passionate Customers Are Loyal Customers

"If you look back 100 years from now, history will show that Whole Foods will be in the top five companies that changed the world."

—DOUG GREENE, FOUNDER, NATURAL FOODS MERCHANDISER

When organic- and natural-foods supermarket Whole Foods Market opened its new, 59,000-square-foot store in New York City's Columbus Circle, eager shoppers were literally lined up around the block waiting to get in.

For groceries.

Manhattan is a mecca for food—fresh, cooked, processed, packaged—hundreds of kinds of food are available on virtually every street corner. The city has dozens of specialty markets and hundreds of places to buy fresh produce and high-quality groceries.

So what drove Manhattan's famously impatient consumers to wait on line to buy their groceries? What is so special about Whole Foods? We believe that the company exemplifies all the principles of the Loyalty Factor: employee loyalty, customer loyalty, and brand loyalty. In making the three work together seamlessly, Whole Foods has achieved the type of loyalty that we would like to see every company achieve.

Whole Foods CEO, president, chairman, and cofounder John Mackey began his business as a small health-food store in Austin, Texas. He opened his doors to his first customer in 1978. Today, Whole Foods Market is a $3-plus billion corporation with, at this writing, 26,000 employees and over 150 stores in the United States, Great Britain, and Canada. That makes Whole Foods the largest organic- and natural-foods grocer not just in the United States, but in the world.[5]

Mackey is passionate about food—food that is good, fresh, ethically raised, and, in the case of animals, humanely treated. Journalist Charles Fishman, writing in *Fast Company*, says that Mackey "has done more to improve the quality, sustainability, healthfulness, and purity of the food Americans eat—from farm field and barnyard to kitchen table—than anyone else in the past 25 years."[6]

Mackey's philosophy is to treat people—and animals, and the

earth—fairly. (This is similar to Southwest Airlines's embrace of the Golden Rule: Treat others as you would like to be treated.) He believes in sharing information with staff members (called team members) and customers alike, going so far as to invite customers to visit the farms where Whole Foods chickens are raised.

Mackey's passion is shared by his employees. They believe in the company's mission and the value of what they do. As a company document states, "In addition to receiving fair wages and benefits, belief in the value of our work and finding fulfillment from our jobs is a key reason we are part of Whole Foods Market."

That statement comes from a manifesto called the Declaration of Interdependence, written in 1985 by a group of sixty Whole Foods team members. The Declaration embodies the company's formal mission statement; it's been updated several times, but the essentials have remained the same. The Declaration spells out the company's vision, its goals—including both customer happiness and team member satisfaction—and how it plans to meet those goals. You can find the Whole Foods Declaration of Interdependence on the company Web site.[7]

It All Begins with Employee Loyalty

"We're creating an organization based on love instead of fear."

—JOHN MACKEY

In January 2004, Whole Foods employees rated their company as one of *Fortune* magazine's "100 Best Companies to Work For"— for the seventh year in a row. Whole Foods was the only national supermarket retailer named, and one of only twenty-four companies to make the list every year since it began.

In a company statement, John Mackey underscored the fundamental relationship between satisfied employees and company growth. "My business philosophy since I began this company more than 23 years ago has focused on the fundamental importance of Team Member happiness," Mackey said.

> *The job of the company's leadership is to empower Team Members and to help them learn, grow, and flourish. Along with our great performance for 2003, making the Fortune list once again illustrates that our everyday aspirations to be one of the best companies in the country to work for go hand in hand with our business success and shareholder satisfaction.* [8]

Whole Foods has a culture of democracy, consensus, and open communications. As at Semco SA, new employees must be approved by a majority of their would-be colleagues; any employee who is curious about how his pay relates to that of others can simply open the binder that exists in every store and see who got paid what in the previous year, from John Mackey on down.

Compensation is also democratic, certainly compared to that in most corporations. Top executives earn no more than fourteen times the average pay of team members in the retail stores; in addition, employees are eligible to receive stock options, and all but 6 percent of stock options go to nonexecutive employees.

Like Rackspace's Rackers, Whole Foods team members operate, well, in teams, with each person sharing responsibility for the group's success. Teams have monthly meetings to discuss such questions as hiring new employees or confirming a hire. Each team's compensation is directly linked to how well that team functions. Each month, team performance is measured in terms of overall productivity; profit sharing based on those numbers is added directly to each team member's paycheck.

Like the associates in Best Buy's customer-centric stores,

Whole Foods team members have a fair amount of control over what their store stocks, based on customer preference, and even how the store looks; there is no standard Whole Foods blueprint for a store. Rather, each location is designed by a team selected by the regional manager.

The company recognizes the importance of every staffer, even those without customer-facing responsibilities. And it's not just about money—there's mutual respect. Like Eastern Bank, the company has instituted a policy of showing appreciation for colleagues. Before a business meeting can end, for example, everyone in the room is asked to mention something he appreciates about one of the other people in the meeting.[6]

Employee Loyalty Drives Customer Loyalty, Which Drives Brand Loyalty

"Customers experience the food and the space, but what they really experience is the work culture. The true hidden secret of the company is the work culture. That's what delivers the stores to the customers."

—CHRIS HITT, FORMER PRESIDENT, WHOLE FOODS

Whole Foods clearly recognizes the link between its employees and the customers they serve—and it recognizes the benefits. As the Declaration of Interdependence states: "We go to extraordinary lengths to satisfy and delight our customers. We want to meet or exceed their expectations on every shopping trip. We know that by doing so we turn customers into advocates."

When *Child* magazine sent a panel of experts to evaluate supermarkets throughout the country, it became a very visible advocate for Whole Foods. In July 2003, the magazine named Whole Foods one of America's ten top supermarkets for families.[9] The magazine cited the Whole Foods roster of children's activities; kid-friendly organic food, including applesauce, peanut butter, and pudding; the "food safety training" required of all managers; and that no Whole Foods products contained any "preservatives, artificial ingredients, flavorings, additives, or trans fats."[10]

Customers' advocacy has a direct impact on the company's financial results. Same-store sales increased almost 9 percent in 2003, topping a consistent record of same-store growth every year in the last five years. On average, each Whole Foods store increased its sales by over 40 percent between 1999 and 2003. As impressive as that is on its own, consider that the rest of the grocery industry posted overall growth of 13 percent over a similar period. Investors aren't left out: In May 2004 Forbes.com said that Whole Foods was "among the most attractive healthy-living stocks. . . . Its products are healthy, environmentally friendly and highly profitable."

A Core Plan for Success

Semco SA, Dell, Best Buy, Rackspace, Eastern Bank, Southwest, Staples, Lowe's, KitchenAid, and Whole Foods: These and other companies that exemplify the Loyalty Factor have several core strategies in common:

1. *Honestly assess your company's present situation, and target your stress points.* When Ricardo Semler experienced his near heart attack, he realized that his organization had to change. He began by examining his biggest stress point—himself—and realigning the company to work more independently.

2. *Create focus and strategy through shared vision, values, and positioning.* Dell has been performance focused since its earliest days. When the tech crisis came, the company stuck

to its use of performance metrics but added measures to gauge employee progress and satisfaction.

3. *Use communication to develop credibility and support.* Whole Foods provides ongoing, substantive communication to employees and to customers, stockholders, and other stakeholders, supporting the company's commitments to its core values.

4. *Establish an infrastructure for success.* Eastern Bank gives its managers the ability to acknowledge employees right on the spot, with "bonuses" like gift certificates to reward and motivate excellence. The company strives to recognize each and every employee's contribution, not just from management's point of view, but through the votes of fellow staffers, culminating in an annual event to honor outstanding employees.

5. *Foster ongoing success through continuous evaluation and feedback.* Rackspace changed its company culture from isolated individualism to cohesive teams with measurable responsibility for customer satisfaction, as well as the team's collective compensation.

Of course, each of the companies we've examined follows more than one of these strategies. In fact, each of these strategies is crucial for creating and maintaining the Loyalty Factor.

Following these five steps will help your company achieve the Loyalty Factor's three-pronged goal: employee loyalty, customer loyalty, and brand loyalty.

All you have to do to get started is turn the page.

PART 3

CREATING THE LOYALTY FACTOR

8

Five Essential Steps to Productivity and Profitability

"Throughout the centuries there were men who took first steps, down new roads, armed with nothing but their own vision."

—AYN RAND

Employers and employees have two very different views on company loyalty. According to Randstad North America, whereas 65 percent of workers say that they are loyal to their employers, only 41 percent believe that loyalty goes two ways. Employers have an almost mirror-image view: About 70 percent say that they are loyal to their employees, whereas only half say that their employees are loyal in return.[1]

The survey suggests how important loyalty is to employees and employers alike . . . and highlights the disappointments on both sides. Although the numbers show everyone's desire for loyalty, the truth is, people don't always see it, or feel it, for themselves. Loyalty is like love: For a relationship to work, the feelings must be mutual.

The good news is that understanding the need for loyalty and wanting loyal feelings reciprocated creates an environment that is ripe for change—an environment that is ready for the Loyalty Factor.

We've discussed a number of companies that put elements of the Loyalty Factor in place, reaping the rewards of higher employee satisfaction, customer loyalty, and brand loyalty. Going beyond those success stories is the next part of our journey.

In the course of our work with hundreds of companies, we've observed the elements that work best to help companies and employees alike achieve the mutual loyalty that clearly most of us prefer—and that characterizes a breakthrough company, with loyal employees, loyal customers, and a loyal brand following.

How can your company create the Loyalty Factor?

"We're not selling our products, we're selling our people."[2]

—ELISABETH B. ROBERT, PRESIDENT AND CEO,
VERMONT TEDDY BEAR COMPANY

In the course of our work, we've found that there are five Essential Steps that any company can implement to create and foster increased loyalty among its employees, customers, and other stakeholders. This unique process, developed by organizational psychologists, veteran marketers, and others, fuels momentum and trust by engaging and valuing every constituency in an organization, at every level, within every department.

The five Essential Steps are a structured approach for developing individuals' commitment to the company's mission and vision. They transcend industries, company size, and geography; they are effective on any scale, from developing greater loyalty between a single manager and her direct reports to implementing a global change process within a major multinational.

Companies that implement the five Essential Steps find that employee loyalty is greater, customer loyalty is firmer, and brand loyalty fuels the company's continuing growth and sales. In short, these Essential Steps lead your company directly to your destination: the Loyalty Factor.

The Loyalty Factor's Five Essential Steps to Productivity and Profitability

Step 1: Assess your company's present situation and target your stress points.

Step 2: Create focus and strategy through shared vision, values, and positioning.

Step 3: Use communication to develop credibility and support.

Step 4: Establish an infrastructure for success.

Step 5: Foster ongoing success through continuous evaluation and feedback.

As we explore each step in the following chapters, keep in mind that, like any long-term change, the Loyalty Factor is most successful when you develop and commit to a long-term process of change and change management.

Let's begin.

9

The First Essential Step:

Assess Your Company's Present Situation and Target Your Stress Points

"Most of our assumptions have outlived their uselessness."

—MARSHALL MCLUHAN

In its study "Working Today," the consulting firm Towers Perrin discovered that 78 percent of the employees surveyed wanted their employers to succeed and were willing to work harder to help the organization reach its goals.[1]

And yet, how many of these employees felt "highly engaged" by their job or their company? Only 17 percent—fewer than one in five. Worse, a greater number—almost 20 percent—claimed to be disengaged, while the balance, two-thirds of those surveyed, described themselves as just "moderately" engaged.

Similarly, Kathleen D. Ryan and Daniel K. Oestreich, authors of *Driving Fear out of the Workplace,* found that although almost all of the employees at the 350 companies they surveyed wanted to do what was best for their organization, seven out of ten held back from contributing their ideas. Why? They were afraid that either they would be ridiculed or no one would be interested.[2]

Why is it so critical for employees to feel engaged? Among other benefits, engagement is a key building block for employee loyalty. According to the Gallup Organization's Q12 research, which included surveying more than ten thousand business units in fifty-one organizations, highly engaged employees are more loyal—and create more loyal customers.

Gallup found that highly engaged employees offer their employers a number of tangible benefits, including increased productivity, employee retention, customer retention, safety, and profitability.[3]

Employees in the nonprofit sector tend to feel more engaged than their private-sector counterparts; the Towers Perrin survey reported that 42 percent of workers in not-for-profit organizations said that they felt highly engaged. One logical explanation for this is the connection that these employees often have with their organizations' purpose and the satisfaction that comes from being part of a worthy cause.

Executives across the board often feel far more engaged than their employees. What do they have that other employees often do not? One answer, according to Towers Perrin's report, is the amount of challenge many executives find in their jobs and the influence that they have in their companies.

What does this tell us about the key drivers of employee engagement and loyalty? *Personal challenge. Influence. Sense of mission. Personal connection. Satisfaction.* These are the feelings we want to instill in a broader range of employees, below the executive suite and beyond the nonprofit sector. These feelings, this sense of being highly engaged, are hallmarks of the Loyalty Factor at work.

Behind the solid statistics about improved business results are the soft truths about human feelings and psychology. Employees who are valued for their work, who are trained to do their jobs in a manner consistent with the company and brand values, who are inspired and encouraged to take on new responsibilities, and who are treated with respect will be more fully engaged in their jobs and happier at work.

When you think about it, isn't this really just simple human nature? These are the same principles we follow in our private lives. We trust those who trust us. Friendships and partnerships are built on mutual respect.

Discovering the Disconnect

"Even if you're on the right track, you'll get run over if you just sit there."

—WILL ROGERS

So management and employees don't always see eye to eye—that's nothing new. But this age-old fact can quickly become a problem when management doesn't realize how its actions affect employees.

The first Essential Step of the Loyalty Factor process is a frank, clear-eyed assessment of the current environment. Implementing this honest, no-holds-barred assessment can have a potentially profound impact on the future of your company.

Why is this in-depth evaluation so important? We find that many companies are not awake to inconsistencies in their corporate culture. These can range from diverging opinions about how to manage specific objectives to deep divides regarding fundamental values and core business practices.

Some of the more everyday disconnects may seem familiar; for example:

- The company that claims that it is, or wants to become, customercentric, but doesn't help employees provide the best possible service—whether through training, process tools, management reinforcement, or rewards and recognition

- The company that talks about its "open environment," but keeps management isolated behind closed doors

- The company that says that it values its employees or considers them its greatest resource, but doesn't request or encourage dialogue with the rank and file[4]

In most companies, we've found that these attitudes and practices are like old habits. They're too ingrained and too familiar to be visible, but they're there, working like fissures underneath the surface of the earth, ready to crack wide open under stress. What kind of stress can cause these ruptures to happen? It can be a merger or an acquisition, a new CEO, an economic downturn, a competitive development, a strike, or even a natural (or manmade) disaster.

Companies that have created the Loyalty Factor can ride out these events—perhaps bruised, but not permanently damaged. Others that do not have the goodwill and fundamental loyalty of employees, customers, and other stakeholders may find themselves in situations from which it will be expensive, or even impossible, to recover.

Remember what happened to IBM? For most of the computing era, IBM was the undisputed market leader, selling large, powerful computers to big organizations. Those were the days, if you recall, when computers were large, mysterious, back-office machines, understood and run by only a handful of experts. IBM's market leadership, sterling reputation, and long-term loyalty to employees built up an enormous reservoir of goodwill and trust among customers, shareholders, and employees alike.

In the mid-1990s, however, IBM missed, or, more accurately, sat out, the PC revolution. As companies switched from buying big computers to buying desktop models, IBM lost its footing. In December 1992, the company posted its largest loss in almost eighty years of business; by 1993, IBM was close to bankruptcy.

When Lou Gerstner joined the company as CEO, the industry widely expected him to preside over the breakup of IBM. Instead, he began to turn the company around. Why did he succeed? The market gave Gerstner the latitude he needed, based on the deep, fundamental loyalty that IBM had earned in the past—although there was still a high price to pay for the company's missteps. In the course of restructuring, Gerstner had to let go more than eighty thousand IBM employees, and the company spent literally billions of dollars (almost $9 billion, according to one estimate) on new marketing, infrastructure, and product development, among other major initiatives.[5]

IBM paid dearly for losing loyalty at the beginning of the PC era. More recently, we can look at the infamous example of Jayson Blair at the *New York Times*, a young reporter whose actions brought about the resignations of the paper's top editors and created a loss of trust in news sources across the country.[6] From his first job as a *Times* intern, Blair was quickly promoted; his assignments soon included covering prestigious stories, such as the return of Pfc. Jessica Lynch from Iraq. Although Blair's immediate supervisors flagged serious problems with his work, senior management turned a blind eye to discrepancies in the reporter's stories, a lack of expense reports for stories that required reporting outside New York, and routine errors of fact.

When the scandal broke, as bad as it was, it uncovered a fundamental issue in the *Times*'s newsroom: a lack of employee loyalty to senior editors. Why? According to a report in the *Philadelphia Inquirer*, neither of the two top editors "possessed the loyalty or political capital to sustain them through the scandal."[7] Their management style, Blair aside, had alienated much of the staff, and as Lori Robertson, managing editor of the *American Journalism Review*, observed, "Morale . . . matters. If bosses treat too many of their employees badly, a general lack of support will result."[8]

Whatever the editors' reasons may have been regarding their choices about Blair, as well as the rest of the newsroom staff, the fallout was a huge blow to the *Times*'s reputation, damaging employee morale, forcing a review and overhaul of senior management, and taking the company away from its main business: reporting "all the news that's fit to print."

These aren't isolated incidents, nor do discrepancies have to be dramatic to be damaging to a company's success. Virtually every company we've ever known or worked with has had varying degrees of disconnectedness between individuals and groups within the organization. Targeting these stress points, or areas of disharmony, is the first step in creating positive change.

How does the process start? It's simple: by asking the right questions, engaging employees in the dialogue, and listening to the answers.

"Listening Begins at Home"

"Touching lives, Improving life."

—Procter & Gamble corporate brand statement

Procter & Gamble knows the value of face-to-face communications: It is known for the diligence of its consumer interviews, focus groups, and household research. Employees, however, were another matter. In a case study entitled "Listening Begins at Home" in the November 2003 *Harvard Business Review*, James R. Stengel, global marketing officer of Procter & Gamble, and Professors Andrea L. Dixon and Chris T. Allen of the University of Cincinnati provide a dramatic example of how one of the world's largest consumer goods companies turned around its fortunes—by talking with, and listening to, its employees.[10]

This particular story starts in 2000, a low period for the giant corporation. As the authors describe it, half of P&G's top brands were in decline, the company's stock price had plunged, and "employee morale had been devastated."

Worst of all, perhaps, was the situation in the company's legendary marketing department. In 1998, the company's centralized corporate marketing group, which was vital to the success of brands around the globe, had been virtually decimated in a corporate restructuring. As a result, the company's marketing teams felt devalued, unsupported, and out of touch with the customers whose experiences and feedback had shaped so many P&G products and marketing campaigns.

Determined to reverse the situation, A. G. Lafley, P&G's newly arrived chairman, president, and CEO, turned first to his executive team. There was no shortage of tactical ideas, from creating new training programs to adding another level of management. None of the suggestions, however, was based on solid information about what was really going on inside the company—an approach, ironically, that would never be tolerated for any of P&G's external marketing initiatives.

So, for the first time, using the same consumer research techniques that had launched and grown some of the world's most famous household brands, P&G decided to find out what its employees had to say about the company and what problems and possible solutions they could identify.

"No one ever listened themselves out of a job."
—CALVIN COOLIDGE

The project began with a small core of employees and over the course of six months was extended throughout the entire company; the research also touched some of the company's outside stakeholders and industry observers. At each step, the process provided P&G with specific insights and information that could then be verified and expanded in the next stage.

The research involved six distinct stages:

1. In-depth employee observation, not unlike traditional anthropological research
2. Employee focus groups
3. One-on-one employee interviews
4. Company task force
5. Companywide survey
6. Interviews with outside stakeholders and industry observers

When the final report was presented, management listened to what had been said—which, despite the large numbers of people responding and the diversity of their viewpoints, was remarkably consistent.

As a result, according to the case study authors, the company created "the most dramatic and sweeping redesign of P&G's marketing organization in sixty years."

Within a year, the authors report, employee confidence in the company more than doubled, soaring to 56 percent of those surveyed from a low of 26 percent the year before. At the same time, the company also began to see a dramatic improvement in its business, with virtually all of its top brands reporting increased volume.

The company's commitment to listening didn't stop with this initial research project, as comprehensive as it was. Global Marketing Officer Stengel continues to have conversations with employees, both in P&G headquarters and in offices throughout the network, deepening employee loyalty (and improving productivity) through mutual respect and active dialogue.

Five Key Questions Every Company Should Ask Its Employees

Here are the questions we use to start the listening process:

1. What is your present level of pride in and commitment to this organization?
2. What are the top three strengths of the organization?
3. What are the top three areas needing improvement within the organization?
4. How do you feel you can better contribute to the overall growth, profitability, and customer satisfaction levels of the organization?
5. If you could give one message to senior management, what would it be?

A Strategy for Any Company—and Every Company

"The quality of an organization can never exceed the quality of the minds that make it up."

—HAROLD R. MCALINDON, *LITTLE BOOK OF BIG IDEAS*

Companies with pockets less deep than P&G's can still create a more productive atmosphere, paving the way for creating the Loyalty Factor in their own organizations.

The guiding principle of the first Essential Step of the Loyalty Factor is for management to create and sustain a meaningful conversation with its employees. This doesn't require an enormous outlay of money; what it does require is a strong commitment. The Loyalty Factor works when managers at every level, starting from the top, actively challenge and encourage staff throughout the organization to contribute their thoughts, ideas, and creative solutions for making their jobs, their department, or the company run faster, better, and more efficiently.

As part of our discovery process, we often poll employees to find out how they rate their managers. We recently received an unusually high rating for a top-level executive at an international Internet service provider; We dug deeper to find out what made this manager so efficient and so well respected by his staff. Here is what they said:

"He works from the positive. He is ethical, compassionate, and helps others achieve their goals," one team member said.

One woman wrote that she admired her boss because "he leads by example but doesn't direct us. He'd never ask us to do something he wouldn't do."

A third wrote, "He is honest and up front. I trust him and want him to respect me and my work."

Finally, one reviewer highlighted perhaps the greatest strength a manager can have: "He knows what he is not good at and finds help in those areas. He distributes the power and gives credit where credit is due."

Achieving the respect and loyalty of employees is crucial to the success of any company. This manager earned not only the respect of his team, but also the respect of his superiors as a result of his group's productivity. Customer satisfaction increased under his management as well—from 79 to 93 percent in one year.

Listening to employees and acting on their input has to be encouraged from the top and filter down to the most granular level: between individuals and their peers, direct reports, and managers. It isn't a coincidence that the greatest loyalty in companies today is between team members. Companies that implement the Loyalty Factor successfully take advantage of this powerful trend to help employees in every corner of the organization understand the vision, values, and strategic direction of the company—and become more loyal to their colleagues, as well as to the company itself.

How do they do it? Let's turn to the second Essential Step.

10

The Second Essential Step:
Create Focus and Strategy Through Shared Vision, Values, and Positioning

"Culture does not change because we desire to change it. Culture changes when the organization is transformed; the culture reflects the realities of people working together every day."

—FRANCES HESSELBEIN, *LEADER TO LEADER*

The menu was classic French: mussels provençale, salade verte, steak au poivre, and crème brûlée. The cooks? Two dozen executives from one of the world's largest financial services firms, demonstrating their expertise at the cutting board and saucepan. All was going according to plan, except for the group preparing the mussels. Everyone on mussels duty was standing around drinking wine—a nice Côte du Rhône—except for one fellow cleaning mussels by himself.

We were creating this feast as part of an exercise to observe and evaluate work habits and how employees interact. So despite the fact that the mussels team was accomplishing its objective, it seemed that there might be a more effective way to go about it.

The man cleaning the mussels explained his strategy by saying, "I told the other guys I could do this better and faster alone, so they should go and have some wine while I took care of it."

Not having to be asked twice, the remaining guys on the team (they were all guys, as it happened) concurred: "He told us we could go drink some wine," one said, "so here we are."

Meanwhile, other teams were chopping, slicing, mixing, and stirring. Had it occurred to the benched men on the mussels team to ask if they could help? It had not. Could they do that?

"I guess so," came one reluctant reply.

It sounded like a reasonable (and satisfying) tradeoff: I'll do the work; you drink the wine. In fact, however, it was a lesson in same old, same old. The mussels cleaner, it turned out, always operated this way. If he could do a job himself, he would. If one of his direct reports did something, it generally wasn't good enough. At the office, as in the kitchen, the rest of his group didn't see any reason to work harder or to try to contribute more: They knew when they weren't wanted or needed.

Nor were they trained or encouraged to look for other opportunities to be productive. Even in the big, open space of a professional kitchen, in clear view of colleagues doing everyday tasks, it seemed perfectly natural to drink wine and chat while others were working.

The result? Each of the other teams had its own reaction to what was happening at the mussels station. There were hints of resentment at the salad station, of scorn at the steak station. Only the members of the dessert team shrugged their shoulders and asked for a bottle of wine to be passed their way, as well.

When the meal was served, the participant-chefs talked with our facilitators about the experience they'd had cooking together. The members of the salad, steak, and dessert groups had enjoyed their team experience but didn't like the dynamic created by the mussels team, feeling that it reflected badly on the whole group and contributed to some ill feelings in an otherwise enjoyable experience.

The members of the mussels group, who should have had a satisfying experience as a result of their consensus on how they would work together, were the unhappiest. Their course received the least praise, although it was delicious, and the majority felt sullen, knowing that they hadn't contributed to the results as much as the other participants had.

The vision of a four-course meal was a delicious reality. The process of creating it, though, had revealed a weakness in the company's values: One person's hard work, even if it met the quota for the whole group, could not make up for the loss in productivity and morale that came from leaving employees sidelined and stranded.

The lesson? Corporate goals are often more abstract than making dinner, but taking action on them is no less necessary. At the end of the day, even if the vision has been made a reality, what was the opportunity cost? What could have been done faster, smarter, and in a way that was more satisfying for all of the participants?

The first Essential Step for creating the Loyalty Factor was to engage everyone in your organization to shape the company's vision and align its stated values with reality. The second Essential Step is to share those values, and that vision, with the same people who helped shape it: your employees.

A Gold Standard

"For employees to treat customers well, the organization has to treat the employees well. Our vision and values were shaped as a way of saying how we want to treat our employees so that they feel respected, and then mirror the positive feelings to our customers."[1]

—BETH SAWI, FORMER CHIEF ADMINISTRATIVE OFFICER, CHARLES SCHWAB

If you're visiting the U.K. and stop in at one of Beaverbrooks, Ltd.'s fifty-two retail jewelry stores, you'll probably be offered a cup of tea while you browse. If you have to wait for a repair, you might be offered lunch, compliments of the house.

Naturally, Beaverbrooks's six hundred employees are well versed in their company's philosophy of providing exceptional customer service. Less expected, perhaps, is that those same employees nominated their company as the best retailer to work for in the U.K.—and won. In 2004, a survey sponsored by the *Sunday Times* of London found that Beaverbrooks was rated the best retailer to work for in the country.[2]

Beaverbrooks the Jewellers, Ltd. was founded in 1920 by three brothers; the company is still family owned. Managing director Mark Adlestone, a grandson of one of the founders, has a vision of "family" that includes every member of his team, from the stock clerks to the senior staff. He makes it a point to know each of his employees by name—aided by a giant wall chart featuring a mini-profile of every employee in every store.[3]

The company has created a culture of appreciation and openness. About 85 percent of the employees report that their managers express appreciation for their work on a regular basis and care about their job satisfaction. Almost 90 percent of the employees agree that their managers are open and honest with them, and most feel that their managers do more listening than instructing.

In addition to the personal touch (how often does a CEO remember a shop clerk's name?), the company has a distinct program to recognize and reward employees and show them how much they're valued. Employees are provided with in-house training and are encouraged to pursue professional training in jewelry knowledge or jewelry sales skills. Employees who successfully complete a management development program receive both a bonus and a trip to London, where they're treated to dinner with Adlestone.

Does working for a jewelry company have great perks? Well, yes: Staff benefits include a 25 percent discount, which can go as high as 40 percent for long-term employees. Once a year, each employee can buy one expensive item (valued at £500 or more) at half price.

Even more important, Beaverbrooks offers employees the chance to feel that they have a role to play in the company's success. The company has a policy of promoting from within: Its top five executives have been with the company for more than twenty-five years, and fifty out of fifty-two managers came up through the ranks. Employees share responsibility for their department's sales results, and everyone whose suggestions contribute to new developments within the company is eligible for one of a series of rewards.

Just as Adlestone takes pride in his family heritage and the company his family founded, Beaverbrooks's employees have a similar feeling: Some 88 percent say they're proud to work for Beaverbrooks.

Shared vision, shared values. Both within the company and when dealing with customers, Beaverbrooks has many of the best qualities you'd expect to see in one big, happy family.

Shared Vision, Shared Results

"If we habitually focus on how to improve things that are already great, can you see how this spirit can transform ourselves, our organizations, families and communities?"

—TONY ROBBINS

In its business model, IHOP (formerly known as the International House of Pancakes) could hardly be more different from Beaverbrooks's family-style operation. Once a favorite for its silver dollar pancakes, among other signature foods, by the 1990s IHOP had become more a real estate developer than a restaurant owner, building and selling new stores, yet controlling only about 10 percent—despite the fact that every restaurant bore the IHOP name.

By 2000, the company was in the doldrums. When president and CEO Julia Stewart arrived in December 2001, she found a company that was fragmented and disorganized. The powerful IHOP brand (once so meaningful to American consumers that the company had followed the public's lead in shortening its name) had lost much of its meaning. Franchisers, who owned and operated 90 percent of IHOP's more than eleven hundred locations, ran each restaurant as an individual enterprise.[4] Every restaurant had its own character and its own version of service, speed, and quality.

Stewart's immediate problem, however, seemed to be financial: The company's largest shareholder was negotiating for cash back to investors, as a result of the company's less-than-stellar returns in previous years.

Although Stewart made the financial model part of her agenda for change, she had a broader vision: to take a much-loved feature of the American landscape, a paradigm of comfort food to millions of Baby Boomers, and not only restore its luster as a national brand, but make it the number one family restaurant chain in the country.[5]

Stewart spent much of her first year at the company talking with, and listening to, employees and franchisees about the current state of the business. She tasted her way through six or seven meals a day at different franchise locations—and even found out what her kids' favorite IHOP dishes were.

Stewart also commissioned extensive customer research. Not surprisingly, the firm learned that customers expected friendly service; minimal waits for a table; and a satisfying, freshly cooked meal. More than that, however, customers seemed to want the comfortable feeling of a local diner, where the staff says hello and good-bye and the waitress stops for a little chat while she pours the coffee. Under the system Stewart inherited, sometimes they got it and sometimes they didn't . . . and each experience would affect whether that customer would walk into any IHOP again, anywhere.

Stewart's investment in engaging her team, listening to the answers, and researching her stakeholders paid big dividends. The challenge that lay ahead only sounds simple: Stewart saw clearly that her task was to create a unified brand from a fragmented organization. In order to meet her goal, she instituted a series of changes that would alter the company's basic structure as well as its culture. Franchisees would still be partners, but they would no longer run their locations on a decentralized basis. Management would create standards and enforce them. And most important, everyone in the IHOP organization would get the tools needed to create the best possible customer experience—one that would be consistently high, and consistent with the brand values, in every location.

How did Stewart communicate her vision to the people who would bring it to life? The most critical element was a training program that focused on the brand's strengths and gave every employee both an in-depth understanding of what IHOP offers its customers and a clear view of each person's role in implementing Stewart's vision of a revitalized company. Employees learned hospitality skills, from greeting diners at the door to recognizing who was in a hurry, to making small talk that is both welcome and appropriate.

The company established nationwide standards for cleanliness, customer service, food quality, and menu offerings and kept a squad of "mystery diners" on the road to ensure that those standards were maintained. The company started promoting its less-known lunch and dinner items, in addition to its famous breakfasts.

Today, the restaurants still serve sixteen varieties of pancakes with those wonderful carafes of flavored syrups. Now, however, each element of the organization contributes to the performance of the whole. Stewart's leadership and vision paid off: True to the company's slogan, customers "come hungry, leave happy."[6] By the end of 2003, same-store sales were up almost 5 percent—the company's best performance in a decade. Franchisers have offered to build the next generation of stores, taking the burden of cash flow and investment away from the parent company.

And that unhappy investor? As it wrote in an SEC filing: "We believe that IHOP is now in excellent hands and that management has established a foundation with meaningful growth opportunities."

Julia Stewart's work with IHOP is a model of the second Essential Step of the Loyalty Factor: creating focus and strategy through a shared vision, values, and positioning. It's a critical element for employees: When Right Management Consultants asked 3,500 "high-value talent" individuals from twenty-six organizations in a variety of industries what makes them choose to join, stay, grow, and contribute to their companies, their single most important answer was the quality of the organization's values and culture.[7]

E Pluribus Unum (Out of Many, One)

"People who work together will win, whether it be against complex football defenses, or the problems of modern society."

—VINCE LOMBARDI

Even organizations that are culturally diverse often have more in common than not.

CarePlus, a New York–based HMO, is a community-based prepaid health service plan that serves the Medicaid population in the New York City boroughs of Manhattan, Brooklyn, Queens, and Staten Island, as well as Putnam County in upstate New York. The company prides itself on hiring staff who mirror its customers' diversity, native languages, and values.

In 2003, CarePlus was only seven years old but had already grown to serve 95,000 members. As employees came to work on August 1, 2003, however, they received some devastating news: The president and founder of CarePlus, whose vision and dedication had brought the company so far, so fast, had died unexpectedly.

The company reins were handed over to Karin Ajmani, the former executive director. Facing a grieving staff, and a critical juncture in the company's history, Ajmani knew that the company needed to regroup in order to get its bearings and continue its growth. The company's next annual retreat for all employees was only weeks away. Although the agenda had been set, Ajmani decided that there was no better time to create the company's first formal mission statement—and to engage everyone in the organization to help.

The first morning of the staff retreat was a Thursday. With all of CarePlus's four hundred employees assembled in a hotel ballroom, Ajmani announced the new agenda and committed to having a fully crafted mission statement by the close of the session—the next business day.

Thus was the staff of CarePlus charged with crafting the vision and creating the future of their company.

Each employee was assigned to one of twenty teams, with each team including people from a wide variety of departments. One group, for instance, included the company's key compliance officer, two members of the housekeeping staff, two people from information technology, nine marketers, two member services representatives, and three company drivers.

There was another challenge: Within this group alone, three spoke Spanish, but little or no English. One Chinese man could speak but not write English. Several others were bilingual in Spanish and English. One spoke four languages—English, Spanish, French, and Creole.

Each team was asked to consider the following questions:

- As a company, what is it that we believe?
- What are we in business to do, and what do we do exceedingly well?
- What is unique about the way we do it?
- What makes CarePlus special or innovative?
- What makes CarePlus a great place to work?

As the teams broke up into smaller conversational groups, they talked about such issues as accessibility and affordability. They focused on quality and responsiveness. They emphasized families and children and communities.

The more they talked, the more personal perspectives emerged. The Spanish-speaking contingent wrote notes on their flip chart in their native language. They emphasized that CarePlus employees treat customers well because of the supportive and respectful way they are treated by their managers. A representative from the marketing department expressed his admiration for the way CarePlus does its work: one child, one family, one community at a time.

The teams' notes were assembled that night. Ajmani and her team set aside the following morning to wade through the input and develop a draft of the mission statement. On Friday afternoon, the ballroom of the Rye Town Hilton in Rye, New York, was filled to capacity. Ajmani told the group that assembling the mission statement hadn't taken all morning; it had taken one hour. "There was so much alignment in all the input," Ajmani told the assembled employees, "that it was easy."

The CarePlus Mission Statement

We provide health insurance, preventive care education, and compassionate care to those with important health care needs. We do this by going the extra mile to develop trusting relationships with our diverse communities. We strive to reach every family we can serve. We are dedicated to making dreams come true—one child, one family, one community at a time.

Source: CarePlus.

As Ajmani read the new mission statement aloud, the sense of pride in the room was palpable. Different groups heard their words and their distinctive phrases spoken or reflected in the formal statement.

What followed was truly remarkable. Eight CarePlus employees joined Ajmani on stage. One after the other, representatives from the marketing, accounting, and provider relations departments stepped forward, reading the new mission statement in their native languages. The audience heard the new mission statement read first in French, followed by Spanish, Russian, Polish, and Japanese.

By the time the last employee finished speaking—in Hindi—the applause was deafening. Tears were flowing. People were on their feet, clapping and laughing and crying all at once.

The company had come together to create a single vision from a diverse universe of viewpoints—a vision that united the company's employees to move forward with a new commitment to growth and service.

By September 2004, the company had welcomed another 16,000 members, an increase of almost 17 percent from the year before. It is clear proof of the power of partnership at CarePlus, where the mission and values belong to everyone.

Every organization has a set of values, and every organization has its own culture: It's the way management treats its staff and how people work together, speak to one another, and show their motivation (or lack of it) in their jobs and attitudes. It shows up in how customers are treated, and whether they return. It's evident in whether shareholders get a fair return on their investments.

Once you've determined that your vision is in line with your employees' and customers' best interests, how do you get your organization on board? How do you help your employees buy in to the vision and make it their own?

That's the subject we'll turn to next, as we examine the third Essential Step.

The Third Essential Step:

Use Communication to Develop
Credibility and Support

"You can't have performance without employee
confidence."[1]

**—JOSEPH D. REID, CHAIRMAN AND CEO, CAPITAL
BANCORP LTD.**

Many years ago, when I was attending a training program
for communications professionals, the instructor introduced the class to an exercise called "paraphrasing." Here's how it
worked. Each of us was assigned a partner, and we were asked to
tell our partners our opinion on a controversial subject. Our partner's job was to say the following: "What I think I heard you say
was . . ." and then paraphrase our opinion in his or her own words.

The first response my partner gave me seemed so far off the

mark that I was sure she hadn't been listening. So my job was to say the same thing again, this time, if I chose, using different words. Again she said to me, "What I think I heard you say was . . ." followed by her paraphrase of my statement.

Eventually, to my great relief, my partner got it "right"—that is, she was able to repeat what I considered an accurate rendition of my original opinion. Then we switched roles . . . and my real lesson began.

Any fleeting thoughts I had had about my partner's intelligence, listening skills, or ability to have a conversation vanished. I too went through multiple rounds of saying, "What I think I heard you say was . . ." before she told me I had finally succeeded in understanding her.

The lesson? No matter how clearly we believe we communicate, what matters most is whether the person at the other end of the conversation understands what we are trying to say. Understanding, even in that short exercise, was a profound, enriching, rewarding experience. When I felt I was not being understood or was having trouble understanding my partner, I felt angry with myself, irritated with her, dismissive of her abilities, and completely frustrated.

As it dawned on me that we were both struggling to communicate (even though we were both professional communicators), I felt both compassion and respect for our efforts in working through our negative feelings to reach a satisfying conclusion.

That's when I learned that listening (and understanding) creates credibility . . . and respect. So often we think that communicating means telling, especially when it comes to top-down communications. As we explore the third Essential Step of the Loyalty Factor, we'll see why this strategy is more likely to fail than to succeed in motivating and managing workers—and how company leaders can market (rather than mandate) their positions and goals to motivate their various stakeholders.

A Credibility Gap?

"The biggest problem with communication is the illusion that it has been accomplished."

—GEORGE BERNARD SHAW

In a 2003 survey titled "Enhancing Corporate Credibility," consultants Towers Perrin found that almost half (49 percent) of the respondents believed that their company generally fails to tell employees the truth. Although almost 100 percent of the employees surveyed suggested that they wanted to know the truth about their company and their jobs, they believed that their companies were more honest with their shareholders (60 percent) and customers (58 percent) than with their workers.[2]

Significantly, the survey confirmed that this "credibility gap" is also a function of the generation gap we discussed in Chapter 2. According to the survey, two-thirds of Gen X and Nexter workers believe that their companies' communications are completely honest, whereas only 44 percent of Boomers and Veterans feel the same way.

It isn't just a question of age that makes employees more skeptical; length of service also seems to make employees more dubious about whether management is telling them the truth. The same survey indicated that regardless of age, 59 percent of the people who'd been with their current employers five years or less were satisfied that their companies were honest with their workers; of the people who'd been employed by their companies for more than five years, fewer than half (48 percent) believed that corporate communications to employees were always true.

Are company leaders and top managers aware that their communications skills may have room—significant room—for improvement? According to Randstad North America's 2003 Employee Review, over half of the managers surveyed (55 percent) described themselves as "excellent" communicators, whereas only 35 percent of employees (that is, those on the receiving end of those company communications) gave their managers that rating. Only a brave 8 percent of managers admitted that their communications skills were poor to fair, whereas almost a third (31 percent) of employees graded their managers that way.[3]

Do employers pay a price for this perception? In a word, yes. The Randstad survey found that "employees who rate their employers as excellent communicators have higher morale, are more loyal, more productive, and have more faith in their supervisors and top management than employees with lower opinions of their employers' communications skills."

One of the hallmarks of truly great communicators is that they use more than just language to get their message across. They use demonstrations, firsthand experience, one-on-one interactions, and other tools to communicate the message that they want to give . . . and have accurately received.

Show and Tell

"Perks are nice, but employees are looking for something more basic. They want to be told the truth, especially if the news is bad. They also want, corny as it sounds, to feel they make a difference and to be given the chance to grow."

—ROBERT LEVERING AND MILTON MOSKOWITZ,
THE GREAT PLACE TO WORK INSTITUTE

Patients at Griffin Hospital in Derby, Connecticut, might be excused for wondering if they're in a "real" hospital. From the elegant lobby to the Jacuzzis, with fresh muffins, live music, and waterfall sculptures, Griffin has created an environment conducive to healing mind, body, and spirit.[4]

It wasn't always like that. Twenty years ago, Griffin was one of several local hospitals competing for the same pool of patients. With admissions and revenues declining, the hospital staff surveyed both the surrounding community and the hospital's own employees to determine what would bring more patients their way.

The responses gave Griffin a new direction, leading to a redesign not only of the physical amenities the hospital offered, but of how it cared for and communicated with its staff.

The primary order of business was to provide patients with an unparalleled level of care and service. Part of the strategy involved physical changes in the hospital's architecture, furniture, and lighting, including not only public areas but patient rooms. Another part of the strategy was to keep patients in contact with their families, with unrestricted visiting hours and family-friendly lounge areas. The hospital instituted more open communications between all the members of a patient's caregiving team, including shared access to medical records and mandatory caregiver conferences.

A fourth part of the strategy (and a critical one) was to create an environment that would allow caregivers to do their best, so that patients would experience the best possible treatment, in every sense of the word. One of the results was a comprehensive program of communications and services for Griffin's staff members, a program that created a culture of open communication and showed employees firsthand what the company's mission was all about.

Every new employee at Griffin goes on a weekend retreat. Spending time with Griffin's president and CEO, Patrick Charmel, and other senior company leaders gives new staff members an in-depth experience of the hospital's philosophy, management, and caregiving style. As part of the hospital's "show and tell" strategy of communication, employees are asked to play the role of patient for part of a day: They're spoon-fed meals, led blindfolded through unfamiliar terrain, and subjected to other unfamiliar, potentially unsettling experiences meant to mirror a patient's feelings as he enters a hospital and begins treatment. The respect and consideration that each "patient" receives from his partners and teammates is emblematic of Griffin's standards of patient care and partnership.

Once on board, employees have no shortage of opportunities to stay up-to-date on Griffin's philosophy, business direction and results, and wellness innovations, or to interact with management.

Every day, employees receive an e-newsletter highlighting what's happening at "Griffin Today." Updates on other important news are sent to employees via e-mail, both at work and at home.[5]

Every month, Griffin's top tier of directors and managers gathers for a leadership conference, in which CEO Charmel discusses the company's marketing, market share, financial performance, business plans, and patient statistics. The attendees share the information they receive with their own staffs, so that every employee is aware of management's priorities, issues, and concerns. In addition, employees are invited to share their concerns, whether about the company, their jobs, or other issues, in a separate monthly meeting.[6]

One of Griffin's tenets for patient care is the notion of a team: Patients are surrounded by a variety of caregivers who share information and responsibility for the patient's well-being. Similarly, Griffin acknowledges every employee's role in contributing to the company's success: Departments that achieve their monthly goals receive a quarterly bonus, and the whole staff is rewarded if the hospital meets its objectives for patient admissions and satisfaction. There are numerous opportunities for individual employees to be celebrated and rewarded for their achievements as well, whether they exceeded their financial objectives or went "the extra mile" for a patient—or even a fellow employee.

Griffin also includes its employees in its philosophy of integrated health and wellness, providing free chair massages, relaxation sessions, and access to a company fitness center. Every year, employees get an opportunity to learn about the latest alternative therapies, such as therapeutic touch, Reiki, and aromatherapy. Employees can sample the benefits of some of these techniques for themselves through a fifteen-minute massage or Reiki demonstration.

There's one other thing Griffin does—a little thing, but one that counts. When an employee, in the course of her normal day, goes beyond company expectations or makes a patient especially comfortable, she might get a little card from her manager, one that simply says, "Thanks."

What has Griffin gained from its open, integrated style? According to *American Hospital Association News*, "Patient satisfaction rates consistently hit the mid to upper 90th percentile. Staff turnover and vacancy rates are well below the regional average, [and] the hospital has seen substantial gains in employee . . . satisfaction and a healthier bottom line."

The hospital has also received numerous awards for both patient care and employee satisfaction. *Modern Maturity* magazine named Griffin one of its "Hospitals with Heart," and in December 2003 Griffin was named one of *Fortune* magazine's "100 Best Companies to Work for in America"—for the fifth year in a row.[7]

The Added Value of Communications Excellence

"Loss of internal communication decreases productivity and speed-to-market."[8]

—J. P. LIEBESKIND, *KNOWLEDGE, STRATEGY, AND THE THEORY OF THE FIRM*

Employees are often more important to your company's success than product, price, or placement. Why? Because they have the ability to delight (or infuriate) customers with every word they speak. And yet, while employees are often measured by productivity, or even customer satisfaction, how much more effective would each of us be—at sales, retention, negotiations, or management—if we were trained in the interpersonal skills, communication skills, and even anger and stress management skills that are such critical assets for today's employees?[9]

When it comes to speaking with colleagues, clients, or other stakeholders, we find that *how* employees—at any level, with any job description—communicate is often more important than *what* they communicate. In face-to-face conversations, 7 percent of the meaning we convey comes from the words we use, 38 percent comes from our tone of voice, and 55 percent is transmitted through physiology—body language. On the phone, as much as 82 percent of the impression that people create is the result of the quality of their voice alone, whereas just 18 percent is conveyed by the words they use.[10]

How do we suggest helping employees learn to communicate more effectively, both internally and externally? Here are three key strategies:

1. *Turn on the tape recorder.* The first thing we suggest is to help each employee understand his own communications style. Listen to the way each employee speaks: Is he upbeat and thoughtful? Does she use customer-oriented language? Is he easy to hear and understand?

We evaluate employees' speaking style, their choice of key words, even their tone of voice. When we play back employees' own words to them on a tape recorder, we find that most people quickly learn how specific elements of their speaking style (words, tone, energy level) affect how they are perceived by those listening to them—and they're eager to know how they can change any negative reactions.

2. *Role-play.* Role playing gives both customer-facing and back-office employees the opportunity to wear the customer's shoes.

It's natural, isn't it? All of us sometimes forget to treat others as we would like to be treated. When employees feel resentful, frustrated, or isolated, it's hard to keep those feelings out of their voices. Putting themselves in the role of the customer often makes it instantly clear that a conversation works best when the employee shows respect for the customer's requests, the customer's time constraints, and in fact, the customer's own communication abilities.

Giving employees insights into the way different customers speak and helping them understand nuances in tone of voice, speaking style, and even word choices can help employees not only speak more effectively, but listen more effectively.

Decoding how people speak and the images they use is another crucial factor in increasing understanding. For instance, did you know that 60 percent of the population is visually oriented? These are the people who talk about "seeing the big picture," or who might say, "That doesn't look right to me." Other people are more inclined to use auditory phrases, such as "I don't like the sound of that."[9] A third group is what we call kinesthetic, who operate in a more emotional landscape. These are the people who might say, "That doesn't feel right to me."

In our experience, once people are aware of verbal cues (which, of course, are the only input available on the phone), they have a better opportunity to give both themselves and the customer a better experience on every call.

3. *Create a sense of belonging—to the work group, the company, and the brand.* Teams are generally more resilient than individuals: We all feel more secure, more confident, and more empowered when we belong to a group that understands and shares our experiences. A key part of our training initiative is to help employees

bond with one another, creating specific shared experiences that break down individual, interdepartmental, or hierarchical barriers to open communication.

As employees are given the opportunity to spend time together in focus groups or other managed environments, they naturally begin to trade stories and ideas; time and again, we find that they actually help one another learn more effectively. If the employees leave their desks feeling isolated or unsupported, as they often do, when they return to their workstations, they return as a team, able to turn to one another at crucial moments for help, support, information, or encouragement.

> *"The customers' perception of the brand is heavily influenced by their interactions with employees."*[11]
>
> —JONATHAN COPULSKY, PARTNER, DELOITTE CONSULTING

Are communications training initiatives like these successful? We've found that satisfaction scores rise on two fronts.

Employees feel empowered by the training and by the opportunity to create better working relationships with their colleagues. They appreciate the company's initiative in improving their job quality, and their experience at work tends to be more meaningful because they have a better understanding of how to solve customer problems.[12]

Just as important, customer satisfaction rises significantly: In some of our clients' companies, *internal* communications training has improved customer satisfaction scores by as much as 20 percent.

When companies communicate well and help their employees communicate more easily, they pave the way for higher productivity, smoother process flow, more effective use of technology, and a higher degree of customer satisfaction.

All of which brings us to the fourth Essential Step, establishing an infrastructure for success.

The Fourth Essential Step:
Establish an Infrastructure for Success

"Put a good employee in a bad system and the system always wins."

— W. Edwards Deming

As you begin to implement the five Essential Steps of the Loyalty Factor in your company, you may come to realize a fundamental truth: Employee loyalty is a critical aspect of every part of your business.

It's tempting to think that we need to worry about loyalty only among customer-facing employees, or among employees with highly specific or sought-after job skills. In fact, however, no matter how technical your business, no matter how computerized or data driven your company, at the end of the day, human beings build and run the machinery, write the programming code, maintain the building, and make sure the bills are paid.

The fourth Essential Step of the Loyalty Factor is to redefine the meaning of your company's infrastructure. This is no longer just a term for your facilities—buildings, plumbing, electricity, networked communications, wires, pipes, and insulation. The infrastructure of the Loyalty Factor rests on three pillars:

1. People

2. Process

3. Technology

Whether your company caters to global enterprise organizations or to small-business owners, to moms and dads or to IT professionals, the employees who develop, run, maintain, and improve your processes and technology are your key asset in gaining, maintaining, and growing customer loyalty—to your company, your products, and your brand.

A New Take on Software

"What helps people helps business."

—LEO BURNETT

For over one hundred years, The International has made its mark in the world of golf. Nestled in the bucolic New England countryside, this private club has devoted its energies to the pursuit of its vision: the creation of a center of golfing excellence.

In the 1950s, the club introduced The Pines, designed by Geoffrey Cornish and redesigned by Robert Trent Jones, Sr. At 8,325 yards, this eighteen-hole course is listed as the world's longest in the *Guinness Book of World Records*.[1] As the club approached its first century, it commissioned designer Tom Fazio to create The Oaks, another eighteen-hole marvel. Upon its completion, not only did The Oaks rank among *Golf Digest*'s top ten best new private courses in America, but it also turned The International into the only thirty-six-hole private course in New England.

The club's state-of-the-art golf academy was also designed with golfing excellence in mind. Cited by the *New England Journal of Golf* as "one of the finest practice facilities anywhere," the twelve-acre site offers 55,000 square feet of teeing area, six target greens, two short game areas featuring four putting greens, and three practice bunkers.

The facilities are only part of The International's formula for success. "Our facilities are the hardware," said Brian Lynch, the club's general manager, "but our people are the software."

The International's goal was to create a premier golf experience for each and every guest. As part of the club's infrastructure for success, Lynch developed a deceptively simple-sounding strategy: From the time of arrival to the time of departure, Lynch wanted each guest addressed by name ten times.

Once Lynch made this expectation clear to his employees, the impact was immediate. Employees discovered that guests were delighted by the feeling of personal attention, and this motivated them to do even more to enhance each guest's experience.

What could be more natural than to call a guest by name? And yet, as in golf, a seemingly basic move took insight to implement and commitment to follow through.

But what about companies that have more complex problems, whose infrastructure has been in place for years? How do you evaluate what's really working and determine which changes will be most effective for solving the company's business issues?

An *Information Week* survey of business-technology professionals revealed that infrastructure problems often boil down to "complex and confusing processes" and "complex and archaic legacy systems."[2]

How can a company's infrastructure be improved or fixed? There's one way to find the answer: Turn to your employees.

An In-Depth Infrastructure Appraisal

"Empowering people to be instruments of development and change benefits a company's bottom line."

—JENNIFER ZAINO, *INFORMATION WEEK*

A few years ago, we came across a small manufacturing company that specialized in refurbishing circuit boards. The company was in trouble: Its revenues were down, employee morale was low, and productivity was lagging. Something had to change. The problem was, the company didn't know what the real problems were.

Starting with Step 1 of the five-step Loyalty Factor process, we used a combination of techniques to evaluate the company's situation and help it figure out what was broken and how it could be fixed.

The situation the company leadership described to us was of a company in a downward spiral. The leaders understood that the company's people felt neither recognized nor guided; that the key business and manufacturing processes were not well understood throughout the organization; and that as a result, business processes didn't flow properly, productivity was off, and revenues were falling rapidly.

Rather than use trial and error to test different incentives or communication tools, they decided to find out what their employees had to say about what they were missing and what they needed.

"Talk to people who will be affected by a project. What do they want? Who or what else could be affected? This sur-

vey could be as informal as a one-to-one conversation or as structured as a major market-research study."

—FORREST W. BREYFOGLE III AND DAVID ENCK, *WISDOM ON THE GREEN: SMARTER SIX SIGMA BUSINESS SOLUTIONS*

We began by conducting focus groups to determine what employees observed about the company's strengths and weaknesses, what they personally needed in order to improve their productivity and profitability, and how they'd answer our favorite question: If you could give one message to upper management, what would it be?

We reviewed our report with management in a frank conversation that acknowledged the issues that the employees had raised. After prioritizing the key issues, we chose four initiatives that had the greatest potential for addressing the company's near-term need for greater productivity and profitability.

Our next step again involved employee participation. We created four teams of six to eight people each; the teams were designed to foster interdepartmental communication by including representatives from each of the company's main departments, in this case Testing, Auditing, Quality Control, Production, Warehouse/Shipping, and IT. While management chose the members of each team, we framed the selection as an invitation: Nominees could decline with no penalty.

We visited each nominee in her work area to ask if she wanted to sign on for the project and to make sure that she understood the goals and the commitment involved. We were rarely turned down, in part because the conversation itself was a first step in showing respect for each person's workload and work/life balance, and the potential quality of his or her contribution.

Each team was assigned to investigate one of the four areas highlighted for improvement: processes, rewards and recognition, communications, and training. To ensure a smooth process flow, each team had a peer leader, a sponsor (one of the company's key executives), and a coach from our organization.

We kicked off the project with an all-day off-site meeting for the team members and management. In the morning, the team members learned about team dynamics: why teams work better than individuals, as well as common stress points and ways to manage conflict. Clearly, these were skills that the employees could bring to their jobs, as well as to managing this initiative.

The afternoon was reserved for an overview of the project itself. The teams were introduced to the objectives and deliverables that senior management had agreed upon. Each team was introduced to its executive sponsor, who could negotiate any changes in the assignment on the team's behalf, if needed, and to its coach, who would be a resource throughout the project, providing guidance and direction and, as the occasion called for, playing devil's advocate.

Then each team received its assignment. The process team, for example, had a multidimensional task to:

1. Document the current process of bringing the circuit boards through the factory and into the market

2. Develop recommendations for streamlining and speeding up the process, including identifying any bottlenecks

3. Outline a plan to communicate the new process to everyone in the organization once it was approved

4. Recommend training on new elements of the process, as needed

As the team huddled with its executive sponsor and coach that first afternoon, it began to identify and parcel out individual tasks. The team members set up expectations for what would be delivered the next week and talked about how they would accomplish their goals.

The challenge? Each team had three months to come back with a final deliverable. The team members would meet formally for only one hour a week, and none of their daily jobs were altered in any way. They had to work together, setting up ties between the different departments they represented, and motivate the people back in their own departments to pitch in as well.

The process team had the heaviest set of responsibilities. How did it meet them? Team members analyzed every job function within the company, talking to each person in every department to find out how the job was currently being done and how it could be improved in terms of efficiency, effectiveness, and cost reduction.

At the halfway mark, we held a short midcourse review. Each team shared a quick summary of its progress; management had the opportunity to review and confirm the teams' objectives, strategy, and tactics, as well as provide any new direction that was needed.

Six weeks later, the teams gathered again, along with the full executive staff. Each team delivered a formal presentation of its findings and recommendations, along with potential costs and timing for new initiatives.

What did the process team recommend as a result of its extensive interviewing and research? The recommendations were targeted directly to areas that were slowing down the work flow, including making physical changes on the manufacturing floor, adding to or shifting responsibilities between job functions, creating specific training programs, and creating a whole new set of safety standards.

The level of professionalism, respect, and optimism that the team members demonstrated was a welcome relief to a management team that had been battling low morale and sagging standards. The executive team now had its own challenge: We gave it forty-eight hours to develop an implementation plan based on the recommendations it had been given.

Two days after the final team presentation, the team leaders were back on stage, this time giving the whole company a summary of the problems, process, and findings, and which changes management was implementing. A conference call was set up for employees who worked outside of the main plant, so that everyone in the company had a chance to listen to what had been accomplished and hear how his ideas and observations had been incorporated into the process.

What happened next? As the recommendations were implemented, work flow sped up. Employees became energized. They saw a direct connection between their ideas and contributions and the changes that management had implemented. Productivity rose. Safety improved. Morale improved. And business improved.

And the team members? They were treated to a thank-you dinner and a $30 gift certificate. It wasn't a showy dinner or a large financial reward, but it was enough. The teams felt acknowledged; their members felt that they had been heard and that their work was respected and appreciated by management.

We checked in with the company six months later, to find out whether the changes were still working and to help it keep energy high. We went back to the long list of recommendations the teams had provided; even after all the new systems that the company had put in place, there were plenty of good ideas left. We helped the company identify the next set of priorities from the same learning—and promised to come back every six months to check in again.

A Blend of Passion and Compassion

"The only way you can manage change is to create it. By the time you catch up to change, the competition is ahead of you."

—PETER DRUCKER

Bob Stiller likes coffee. He likes it so much that he started making it himself, as the founder, chairman, president, and CEO of Green Mountain Coffee Roasters (GMCR), of Waterbury, Vermont.

In 1981 the company was a small café in Waitsfield, Vermont—a town with a population of 1,659, more or less.[3] Today, GMCR is a major supplier of organically grown coffee and a leader in the movement for environmentally responsible products and fair trade practices.

The company's growth, in a sense, was organic: As GMCR began supplying requests for coffee from local hotels, its special roast caught on with skiers and other vacationers from around the country, who wanted to buy GMCR at home. The company's wholesale and mail-order business is still the backbone of the organization, which now employs almost six hundred people and has sales of over $116 million.[4]

For its first few years, GMCR, like many growing companies, was balancing growth with growing pains. Then came a moment that virtually every company can relate to: Stiller and his team were trying to figure out how to make the company more profitable. More to the point, Stiller wanted the team to figure out how the company could reduce expenses.

None of the ideas generated that day appealed to the group, and the one proposal that Stiller did approve seemed completely irrelevant at the time. The idea? A couple of employees suggested forming an environmental committee. From that day on, nothing would be quite the same.

The idea of being environmentally conscious was more than a slogan: The employees whom Stiller empowered began to institute changes that literally started to affect the company infrastructure. How? They began by turning out the lights in empty rooms and turning down the heat to save energy (as well as money). Even this relatively simple idea had to be communicated to employees throughout the company and maintained in order to be effective.

The next initiative was more complex: redesigning the boxes that the company used to ship its coffee so that the company spared trees—and saved money.[5]

In the years that followed, GMCR engineered virtually all of its business processes to support its mission. One of the most striking examples of this is how the company sources the beans that create its distinctive coffees.

The company supports coffee farmers through fair trade practices, processing technology, and community development and services, including education, health care, even hurricane relief. GMCR buys a large percentage of its coffee directly from farmers, rather than from consolidators or other intermediaries, ensuring the growers a higher level of profit.

This, of course, required putting the necessary systems and people in place to identify and negotiate with farmers, cooperatives, and wholesalers in a wide range of countries, including Sumatra, Mexico, Costa Rica, Peru, and Guatemala.[6]

"To help the world, we have to be successful. If we help the world and go out of business, we're not going to help anybody."

—BOB STILLER

One of the key elements of GMCR's infrastructure is its Coffee Team, a small, cross-functional group of employees charged with, among other things, evaluating sourcing opportunities in coffee-growing areas around the world. One of GMCR's more recent initiatives is to seek out coffee farms run by growers who not only practice organic, environmentally friendly farming techniques but also provide decent living conditions for their workers.[7]

GMCR doesn't just make its decisions from its airy offices in Vermont. Every year, groups of employees representing every aspect of the business, from the roasting crews to the sales reps, travel to coffee farms around the world to see firsthand how their suppliers manage their operations and to review the quality of the coffee destined for GMCR's roasters. The company even provides Spanish lessons to facilitate communication between its English-speaking employees and the suppliers and workers they meet. When the teams return to Waterbury, they share their experiences with their coworkers, to give everyone at home a taste of their discoveries.

How does all this effort improve employee loyalty and build a business? According to coffee authority Mark Pendergast, writing in *Tea & Coffee* magazine, "People tend to stick with the company—17 employees have been with Green Mountain over 15 years, while nearly 200 of the 575 employees have been with the company for five years or longer."[8]

And while *Business Ethics* magazine ranked GMCR as one of its "100 Best Corporate Citizens," the company is being noted for its business growth as well: In both 2002 and 2003, *Forbes* magazine noted that GMCR was "one of the fastest growing companies in the country."

One of Stiller's key accomplishments has been to create an infrastructure that supports his company's mission—and his employees' development. Stiller's willingness to let employees try out a possibly far-fetched idea led to a wealth of new initiatives that continue to benefit employees, customers, shareholders, and, in this case, the world itself.

Many company leaders hear ideas that sound far-fetched at first. Unfortunately, many of these ideas get sidelined because there isn't a process in place to test them and evaluate the outcome. There's a downside, though: Perhaps one of these out-of-the-box ideas could be the answer to your next business problem. So how do you figure out when to say yes and when to say no? The answer comes in the next Essential Step.

The Fifth Essential Step:

Foster Ongoing Success Through Continuous Evaluation and Feedback

"We are what we repeatedly do. Excellence, then, is not an act, but a habit."

—ARISTOTLE

As business leaders and managers, we live and die by change—in our P&Ls, our operating expenses, our sales, our revenues, and our stock price. We often review our numbers daily—sometimes even more frequently. Web sites measure hits and eyeballs; direct mailers measure response and conversion; TV advertisers measure Nielsen ratings. When the numbers change, we respond—strategically, tactically, quickly—or we go out of business.

In just the same way, we need to continue to evaluate and respond to our employees.

If the first four Essential Steps are critical to building the Loyalty Factor in your company, the fifth Essential Step may be the hardest one of all, because it involves making a commitment to continue the Loyalty Factor process over time.

Remember the Loyalty Factor formula: Employee loyalty drives customer loyalty, which drives brand loyalty. Just as a car needs to be refueled in order to keep functioning, the Loyalty Factor needs to be practiced on an ongoing basis in order to keep your company on track. To continue to derive the benefits of the Loyalty Factor in your company, you need a plan for consistently and regularly evaluating your company's people and processes—employee satisfaction and customer satisfaction—and measuring how these factors contribute to your productivity and profitability. And in a competitive, changing world, you need to use the information you gather to always—always!—seek out ways to improve the way your company functions.

A Quick Call and a Long-Term Relationship

"Business more than any other occupation is a continual dealing with the future; it is a continual calculation, an instinctive exercise in foresight."

—Henry Luce, co-founder, *Time*

Back in 2000, the management team at Kronos Incorporated had some changes in mind. The company, founded in 1977, established itself as a software provider for time and attendance in the 1980s. Over time, the company had begun adding professional services; by 2000, revenues from services had reached 35 percent of the company's total sales.

Company leaders decided that the opportunity was ripe for increasing service offerings. There was one small problem: The group that was most likely to be in touch with current customers was tech support.

Kronos invited us to help the people on its technical support team evolve from service reps to true customer service providers. What's the difference? Typically, the technical engineers and programmers who answered customer calls could pinpoint the source of a problem with a machine, network, or software. They couldn't, however, necessarily hear the degree of weariness in a customer's voice or react in the most appropriate way. What's more, they had little experience in turning a service call into a sales opportunity.

Our first session with Kronos, in 2000, brought us into contact with some admittedly skeptical technical support engineers. As we helped them learn to communicate more effectively during service calls, and then learn how to provide added-value suggestions for their clients, they began to see the potential power of improving their communication styles—and skills.

> *"Determination and commitment to an unrelenting pursuit of your goal—a commitment to excellence—will enable you to attain the success you seek."*
>
> —MARIO ANDRETTI

The company continued to ask us back to extend the training to more of its Global Support staff. What's happened in the four years since that initial training session? The company has not only met but beaten its initial objective to increase service offerings. The technical service staff has grown from four hundred to seven hundred; communications training continues to be an important engine driving employee and client satisfaction. In fact, Kronos's employees nominated their company as one of the "50 Best Places to Work" in Massachusetts, an award sponsored by the *Boston Business Journal*.[1]

When Is a Customer Loyal?

Your customers' answers to two simple questions will help you identify their degree of loyalty to your business and your brand.

1. Are you willing to recommend our company or our product to someone else?
2. Will you purchase from us in the future?

The company has also amassed a long list of customer satisfaction awards, among them the NorthFace ScoreBoard SM Award by Omega Management Group Corp. Winners are required to have consistent customer satisfaction ratings of 4.0 or better, on a scale of 5.0, for an entire year. As of this writing, Kronos has won the award four years running.

Employees recognize that the company is a great place to work; customers recognize Kronos's strengths as a service provider. What more could the company ask?

Revenue.

In July 2004, the company reported that net income for its third quarter of fiscal 2004 had grown 33 percent in the past year, and that revenue had grown 17 percent in the same period, continuing the company's remarkable record of ninety-eight straight quarters of revenue growth.[2] Its fiscal 2003 revenue was just shy of $400 million; according to management consulting firm Cape Horn Strategies, Kronos is the only public software company besides Microsoft to generate profitable growth every year for more than sixteen years.[3]

"Many of the awards we receive are based on the satisfaction of our customers and employees. It is this satisfaction that drives our success."

—JOE DEMARTINO, VICE PRESIDENT OF WORLDWIDE CUSTOMER SERVICE

In 2004 alone, Kronos was named one of the "100 Fastest-Growing Technology Companies" by *Business 2.0*, one of the "Hottest Companies of 2004" by *START* magazine, and one of *The Boston Globe*'s "Globe 100" companies, among other honors.

Kronos's record of success is one of commitment, not just to its customers (as of 2004, including a collective twenty million employees[4]), but to its own staff. As it continues its program of training and empowering its employees, Kronos is a powerful example of the Loyalty Factor at work, with loyal employees, loyal customers, and a thriving brand.

A Commitment from the Top

"For big companies to change, we need to stop thinking like mechanics and to start acting like gardeners."

—ALAN M. WEBBER, *LEARNING FOR A CHANGE*

Kronos focuses its change management on one of the greatest revenue-generating departments in its organization. There are times in a company's life, however, when there is a change that is so monumental that it requires evaluating the entire organization, one employee at a time, to determine individuals' strengths, weaknesses, and leadership potential. Does change like this happen all at once? Of course not—it's a process that can go on for the rest of the organization's existence.

Tyson Foods is the largest meat-processing company in the world. It was already a $7 billion business, and the leading chicken-processing company, when it acquired IBP Fresh Meats, the leading beef processor and number two pork processor, in late 2001.[5]

The changes that the company embraced were enormous, to say the least. Virtually overnight, revenue more than tripled to almost $25 billion in sales in fiscal 2003, the latest figure available as of this writing. The company almost doubled its staff, from 68,000 to 120,000 employees around the world;[6] Tyson's midlevel management team alone became a small army, more than 10,000 strong.

There was also a question of culture. Despite the outward similarities between Tyson and IBP, the two companies had distinctly different business problems, consumer perceptions, marketing strategies, and supply-chain issues. And just as in any merger or acquisition, executives from the two companies had distinctly different ways of doing business.

How was Tyson to manage, train, and identify talent in the new organization? Chairman and CEO John Tyson decided to start from the top.

Tyson took the unusual strategy of assessing its seniormost executives' talents. Partnering with an outside company, the company did a qualitative and quantitative assessment of cognitive and leadership skills among the company officers.

While the research predictably found numerous strengths in the leadership team, it was also able to pinpoint specific skill sets that could be improved. The company then provided each of Tyson's top executives with an individualized program to enhance his management and leadership abilities.

Recognizing the benefits of the in-depth evaluation and personalized training for its most senior employees, the company invested once again. Tyson provided a similar program of evaluation and training for the next tier in its organization: those employees who were in line for promotion to the director level.

The program was working in two distinct, yet vital, dimensions. First, the evaluation, feedback, and training that each individual received enhanced not only her skills but her ability to function more easily in the new organization—a sure strategy for creating employee loyalty at any level.

Second, the program gave CEO Tyson and his HR team the ability to evaluate the company's overall strengths and weaknesses, and to manage for change and improvement in precisely those areas where they were most needed.

The results of each round of the program whetted Tyson's appetite for its boldest step yet: The company decided to offer the same opportunity for evaluation and training to the members of its midlevel management team—all ten thousand of them.

This decision resulted in the need for a new addition to Tyson's HR infrastructure. As Ken Kimbro, Tyson's senior vice president of human resources, described in an interview with HR.com, the company "put together an emerging leader board made up of people . . . from all levels of this organization. . . . There are corporate members, field members, production members, sales members, and managers. . . . We have team members who have long-term tenure and we have others who are relatively new."[7]

The company then invited each of its ten thousand managers to apply to what was now dubbed the Emerging Leaders program. The EL board is responsible for reviewing each applicant's performance history, application, and even letters of recommendation. Once a year, the EL board approves a new group of Tyson employees for the Emerging Leaders program—putting the successful applicants on a fast track to leadership positions within the company.

One of the beautiful aspects of Tyson's EL program is the way it was developed, grown, and expanded throughout the corporation in measured stages. Starting with CEO Tyson's vision, the program began by focusing on the company's immediate need for a strong, committed leadership team. As the individual skill sets of senior executives were identified, each person got a tailored program that would benefit both his own development and the company's overall management style.

"It's not that I'm so smart; it's just that I stay with problems longer."

—Albert Einstein

As Tyson continued to evaluate the success of the program, it continued to invest in its people. As the evaluation and training program gradually expanded further into the company, the goal changed from strengthening senior management to providing a deeper bench of future managers. Finally, Tyson's vision became a part of the company's HR infrastructure, offering a leadership opportunity to every employee who reaches the manager level.

Tyson's EL program helps employees feel more valued and rewarded—and Tyson's customers feel rewarded as well. In June 2003, Sodexho USA, the leading provider of food and facility management services, named Tyson its Commodity Vendor of the Year. What were the criteria that Sodexho used for its selection?

According to a statement by Marc Boesch, Sodexho's vice president for purchasing, "Sodexho's suppliers do more than just provide great products and service to our units—they help us improve the quality of daily life for our clients, customers, and employees."[8]

And why was Tyson honored in particular? Mitch Greenberg, Sodexho's senior director of commodities, offered this statement: "The Tyson team has taken on Sodexho's needs as if they are their own, suggesting new ways to service units at the lowest cost, providing training and helping Sodexho find sales and growth opportunities."

Like Kronos, Tyson's experience is a strong demonstration of the fifth Essential Step of the Loyalty Factor at work. As a company continues to develop loyal employees, those employees help to create more loyal relationships with customers. In Tyson's case, the proof is in the pudding, so to speak: After all, how many customers give their suppliers national awards to prove their devotion to the brand?

Measuring the Bottom Line

When all is said and done, many, if not most, companies want some tangible, bottom-line proof of the Loyalty Factor's effect.

Our clients measure the results of their Loyalty Factor programs in several ways.

Employee Satisfaction

How do clients measure satisfaction? Clearly, some information can be derived from HR tools and performance measures, including turnover rates, length of tenure, and attendance.

As we've said all along, though, the numbers don't tell the whole story; we find that a more actionable level of knowledge is developed in quarterly or annual checkups. What is a typical Loyalty Factor checkup? It might include one-on-one interviews with key employees, one or more employee focus groups, observation of processes and company communications, and a review of the original objectives relative to current performance.

Just like any annual checkup, these reviews occasionally reveal areas that need to be reinforced or identify new opportunities for improvement. Clients can decide whether they want to fine-tune their operations or begin another phase of change.

Most important, we find that checking in with employees at regular intervals continues the goodwill elicited by the five Essential Steps. As a rule, employees are reenergized by the ongoing evidence of their company's commitment to their satisfaction, career growth, and personal development.

Customer Satisfaction

All of our clients, of course, measure customer satisfaction on a regular basis. Once again, the numbers do tell part of the story: Increased sales, repeat sales, and referrals are all solid evidence that customers have had a good experience with your company. Customer satisfaction scores are also excellent, if incomplete, indicators of the health of the relationship.

Companies that are conversant with the principles of the Loyalty Factor, however, also stay aware of clients' feelings about the products and services they receive. Why? To make sure that small failures don't escalate into larger issues. To ensure that quality is consistent across the board, for every customer serviced. To make sure that large-volume purchases are not solely the result of a problem in the market.

Like many companies, our clients use a variety of methods to check in with their customers on a personal basis, including phone calls from company executives to client leaders; focused conversations between the marketing, sales, and support teams and their client contacts; and follow-up calls from customer service to customers to ensure the quality of each interaction.

Brand Recognition

As loyalty is created, nurtured, and grown from within, it ripples outward. Loyal employees, as we've said so many times, drive loyal customer relationships. Customers, in turn, develop a stronger relationship with the brand.

What is so powerful about that brand relationship? Unlike a

purchase based purely on functionality or price, a brand relationship supersedes individual factors and can survive occasional dissatisfaction with an employee, the product, or the service. The brand relationship is one in which the customer trusts that, over time, the brand will fulfill its promise of quality, service, satisfaction, and return on investment.

A New Value Equation

There's something else that needs to be addressed when we talk about measuring success, and success in developing loyalty in particular. In our prevailing business culture, we tend to treat employees as a cost center. As a result, any investment in them is often seen as adding cost upon cost, a sagging weight on the bottom line.

A new model for business is emerging, however, in which employees are viewed as a resource, an asset, and a fundamental engine for company growth. In this new way of thinking, investing in employees is just as important as investing in more traditional assets, and in some cases more important.

As our society becomes increasingly knowledge based, value, in the words of one academic observer, "is based on the perception of customers. It is the creation of value . . . that is the dominant activity of the new economy."[9]

In this new era of value—based on worker knowledge, customer perceptions, and a shrinking base of qualified employees—company leaders have a growing responsibility to evaluate (and quite possibly change) the operating models of their own organizations.

How can leaders leverage the Loyalty Factor to meet the coming challenge? Let's look at that next.

PART 4

PUTTING THE LOYALTY FACTOR TO WORK

14

The Role of Leadership

"Good business leaders create a vision, articulate the
vision, passionately own the vision, and relentlessly drive it
to completion."

—THOMAS HARDY

I t isn't easy.

Market pressures, regulation, rapidly changing technology, media scrutiny, and stakeholder demands—from employees,
shareholders, customers, government officials, and others—are
creating more complex challenges for company leaders than ever
before

And of course, CEOs are being held more and more account-
able for their company's performance. How risky is the top job?
According to management and technology consultant Booz Allen
Hamilton, the rate of chief executive dismissals went up 170 percent between 1995 and 2003.[1]

Given the pressures that the CEO faces, it's no wonder that championing loyalty might seem to be a lower priority than leading the organization toward greater revenue and profitability. And yet loyalty is what drives the success that virtually every company leader works day and night to achieve.

Significantly, the Booz Allen Hamilton study reports that the best-performing chief executives are "homegrown": Even first-time CEOs who were promoted from within had better overall results than outside hires. In another interesting tidbit, the older the CEO, the more likely he was to keep the top job.

This suggests that loyalty plays a twofold role in a CEO's ability to keep the corner office. First, CEOs from within a company can leverage internal relationships and knowledge to boost performance; and second, employees (and the board) are more willing to support a CEO whom they know and trust.

Trust and Loyalty

"When the going gets tough, people tend to revert to the steadfastness and predictability of traditional values: trust, loyalty, and meaningful personal relationships."

—CONNIE GLASER,
THE ATLANTA BUSINESS CHRONICLE

Trust, and the loyalty it brings, is highly influenced by leaders' personal behavior—and how that behavior is perceived.

The 2004 Trust and Loyalty survey by the Society of Human Resource Management (SHRM) and Career-Journal.com, *The Wall Street Journal*'s executive career guide, found that only 27 percent of employees "strongly agreed" that their company's leadership is ethical.

As CareerJournal.com's editor-in-chief, Tony Lee, observed, "As hiring demand continues to improve, it's even more important for top company executives to maintain employee loyalty by demonstrating that they can be trusted to lead their companies through this period of new growth."[2]

"People are coming to grips with the fact that you make your numbers because of the people you employ."[3]

—JAMES E. COPELAND, JR., CEO, DELOITTE TOUCHE TOHMATSU

How do successful CEOs develop and maintain the loyalty that they need if they are to succeed and help their companies prosper? Executives are starting to agree that employees are a key factor in running a successful business. A 2003 survey states, "Across the board, 79 percent of top executives and 77 percent of senior managers agree that wisely managing human capital is 'very' important to the success of an organization as a whole."[4]

What is the secret of loyalty leadership? If there's one strategy that stands out from every other, it's empowerment. Over the years, we've come up with a definition of leadership that applies to virtually every organization we've seen. Being a loyalty leader means being the best that you can be, *and helping others to be the best that they can be*, by providing an environment in which people can grow and achieve.

Leadership consultant (and symphony orchestra conductor) Roger Nierenberg says that in his experience, leaders are sometimes reluctant to empower employees to do their best work. As Nierenberg observed in an interview with the Global Institute of Leadership Development, "The power of an organization lies in the people doing the work and how they interact with each other. The role of a leader is to create the best possible space for this to happen."[5]

Or as author and teacher John Heider writes, "Good leadership consists of motivating people to their highest levels by offering them opportunities, not obligations."[6]

Loyalty Leadership: Taking the Long View

"I'm over the top on lots if issues, but none comes as close to the passion I have for making people GE's core competency."

—JACK WELCH

Texas Instruments's Tom Engibous has seemingly always been one step ahead of the curve. A lifetime TI employee, Engibous joined the company in 1976, right out of graduate school. Today, he is TI's chairman of the board and the company's chief visionary for corporate loyalty—to employees, customers, shareholders, and the community.

This is a role that Engibous has always played to some extent. In 1997, as a newly minted CEO, Engibous divested a wide variety of TI's ailing bread-and-butter businesses and consolidated the company around then-new silicon chip technology. It was a striking move—and it may well have saved the company. As *Business Week* observed, "His timing was impeccable." The new chips—digital signal processors, or DSPs, became the foundation for a dramatic turnaround in company sales.[7]

Competitors weren't far behind with their own DSP offerings, and the technology bust was just around the corner. Even so, like the employees of many technology companies in the seemingly long-ago 1990s, and with the company's new DSP success under its belt, TI employees often had a "take it or leave it" attitude with customers. Problems in execution, manufacturing, and delivery were all easy for company managers to downplay when TI was the only game in town.

As journalist Paul Harris reported in a 2004 case study, "As customers waited in line for its products, TI became more product and technology centric, and admittedly less concerned about its customers."[8]

Engibous had already decided what TI's next move would be to keep its momentum in a changing market, but it wasn't an easy sell. The company's employees needed to be reoriented toward their customers. Many of the people on the executive team, however, fresh from the recent reorganization, weren't ready for another change so quickly.

> *"People are dying to be connected, invited, involved. They don't like having things shoved down their throats in a formulaic way. They show energy and commitment when they can be players and influence an initiative's outcome."*
>
> —KENNY MOORE, KEYSPAN ENERGY

Rather than mandate an unpopular course of action, Engibous and chief sales and marketing officer Jeff McCreary spent several months observing employees' behavior and discussing and negotiating change management strategies with key executives.

Finally, in 2001, two dozen carefully selected executives were invited to a special off-site meeting. For the next two and a half days, they would learn how to refocus on the real engine of TI's growth: the customer.[9]

The training was designed around scripted role-play, based on actual input from TI employees and customers. TI executives played the part of customers at a fictitious company; a group of outside trainers and consultants took on the role of supplier.

The trainers had developed a list of typical TI employee behaviors, including an insensitivity to customer needs. As the training team gave the TI executives a taste of their own medicine, the executives became increasingly frustrated and angered by their inability to get the results required by the team exercise. It wasn't until the debriefing, when they heard their emotions echoed by taped interviews with real TI customers, that the lesson hit home.

How successful was the training program in changing employee attitudes toward their jobs—and their customer relationships? Since that first session, over two thousand TI employees have gone to the company's "boot camp." Employees relish the real-world aspect of the training and give it record-high satisfaction scores.

What was the impact on customers? By 2003, two years after that first small training session, TI was earning awards from some of the same customers who had been unhappy with the company's service. TI's share of the wireless communications chip market went from 12 percent in 2001 to 17 percent in 2003. Its DSP business went from a 40 percent market share in 2001 to a 48 percent share by 2003.

Tom Engibous was prescient about another trend as well: the changing nature of the workforce and the growing need for employee loyalty.[10] Before most of his contemporaries had identified the problem, Engibous had already begun to engineer a solution: At the same time that employees were being trained to provide better service to customers, TI was asking what it could do for its workforce.

Engibous called it a "re-recruiting initiative." Employees were invited to tell management what they needed to have in order to stay happy at TI, whether it was more flextime, a different job, or even a different manager. Rather than wait for dissatisfaction to emerge—when the cost of retention would be higher, if retention would even be possible—the company decided to invest in employee loyalty *before* employees became unhappy.[11]

That forward thinking, the result of Engibous's extraordinary leadership, has had impressive results. With almost $10 billion in annual sales,[12] TI naturally enjoys a prominent place on the *Fortune* 500 list. As evidence of its success in creating employee, customer, and brand loyalty, TI also has the distinction of appearing on three other *Fortune* lists: as one of America's Most Admired Companies, Most Admired Global Companies—and Best Companies to Work For.[13]

TI demonstrates that even the biggest enterprises can forge employee loyalty, and the positive impact that it has on both customer sales and brand recognition.

What about smaller companies? Can leaders of smaller companies develop the Loyalty Factor when their first order of business is often sheer survival in a competitive marketplace?

Abraham Maslow Meets the Loyalty Factor

"In the end, it is the quality and character of the leader that determines performance and results."[14]

—FRANCES HESSELBEIN, CHAIRMAN OF THE BOARD OF GOVERNORS, LEADER TO LEADER INSTITUTE

When Dr. Abraham Maslow developed his "Hierarchy of Needs" model in the 1940s and 1950s, he demonstrated the progression we make from satisfying our tangible, physical needs to fulfilling our more subtle, but equally important, psychological needs.[15]

Why is Maslow's theory important to the discussion of employee loyalty? The more our needs are met, the more loyal we are apt to be. A look at Maslow's five levels of need, from lowest to highest, provides a foundation for asking some thought-provoking, sometimes troubling, but profoundly meaningful questions about what we offer our employees . . . and what we have yet to deliver.

The First Level: Physical Needs

The hierarchy begins here, with our basic needs, including air, water, food, and sleep. Even at this basic level, how many companies have environments with poor air quality? How much demand is there in some organizations or industries for employees to do without sleep for extended periods? To eat unhealthy or unsatisfying meals quickly, or not at all?

The Second Level: Security

The second priority includes physical safety and psychological feelings of being secure.

When you think about your company, are there ways to make your work environment physically safer? Do employees know how to evacuate the building in case of fire? Are there phone chains in place in case of disasters?

When it comes to the more complicated question of emotional security, are there initiatives that management can take to help employees feel more secure in their jobs? Can management provide more information about company policy, strategy, future plans, and vision, so that employees can concentrate on their jobs instead of on an unknown future?

The Third Level: Belonging

Psychologists note that we have a natural tendency to bond in communities—defined by work, common interests, or family. At their best, these groups accept us for who we are and encourage us to be the best we can be.

How can your organization strengthen internal relationships—within work groups, departments, or regions? How can each connection between employees and the organization be developed and improved?

The Fourth Level: Self-Esteem

Maslow defined two types of self-esteem: our own feelings of pride and achievement when we accomplish a task, and the recognition of those around us, which validates our skills and accomplishments.

When employees do their jobs well, do your managers operate on the principle that "no news is good news"? What systems do you have in place to reward and applaud employees for a job well done, an initiative successfully accomplished, a business objective met or exceeded?

For employees who need help in mastering a new skill or work environment, does your company offer them the opportunity to learn how to do their jobs better? To communicate more effectively? To have a thorough understanding of the company's mission, values, products, and services?

The Fifth Level: Self-Actualization

Maslow's highest level of need is self-actualization, defined as the drive to maximize our potential. On the job, self-actualization is simple to describe, but hard to achieve: You know you've reached the level of self-actualization at work when you're happy with what you do; how well you do it; how you're rewarded for your efforts, both tangibly and psychologically; and how you're viewed by your peers and managers.

Like you, when your employees feel self-actualized at work, they don't want to work anywhere else. They excel at meeting and beating their objectives, because their goals and the company's have become synonymous. It's a high bar for company leadership to achieve; it's the ultimate achievement of the Loyalty Factor.

The Key to Small Business Survival

"It's always been our philosophy to be better than the other choices."[16]

—CELESTE FORD, CEO, STELLAR SOLUTIONS

Every year, over half a million people start a business. According to the U.S. Small Business Administration, small businesses employ half of all private-sector employees and contribute more than half of the privately generated, nonfarm gross domestic product (GDP).[17]

Small businesses are also notoriously volatile: Not including sole proprietorships, about 10 percent of small companies fail each year. So how do leaders of smaller companies keep their employees loyal, navigating the road to growth through the inevitable twists and turns that a new company faces?

Like many people starting (or wanting to start) their own companies, aerospace engineer Celeste Ford had spent almost twenty years working for large corporations and wanted to see if she could do what they were doing—only better.

In 1995, building on her career at aerospace giants Comsat and the Aerospace Corporation, Ford founded Stellar Solutions, an aerospace engineering and consulting firm specializing in satellite technology.[18]

What was her vision for the company? As an article in *Winning Workplaces* pointed out, "Ford combined the two elements most likely to be forgotten in the corporate world: flexibility and empowerment."[19] As Ford herself explained to the National Federation of Independent Business (NFIB), "Employees need to feel important, not that they're just filling a slot. People are a critical resource. If you treat them fairly and empower them to have high impact both within your company and with your customers, your company will succeed."

Ford's strategy centers around recognizing each employee's individuality: his or her skills, career ambitions, ideas, personal interests, and family life.

Every employee participates in the company's annual planning meetings, giving each of them a voice in the company's strategic direction and key initiatives. Each corporate goal is translated into tactical terms, including individual and team responsibilities; bonuses are awarded when the objectives are met. The meetings are also an opportunity for employees to discuss their own career aspirations, part of a long-term initiative to help each person achieve his "dream job."[20]

> *"When you put people in jobs they want to be doing, they do them extremely well, and the customer notices."*
>
> —U.S. Air Force Colonel Kris Henley (Ret.), director, National Intelligence Programs, Stellar Solutions

Managing satellite launches is not a 9-to-5 job, but in addition to motivating employees at work, Ford wanted to provide her employees, and herself, with a better quality of life than she'd experienced in her previous career. A wife, a mother of three, and an active member of her community, Ford was determined to create an environment that would allow people to blend demanding, often unorthodox work schedules with personal life and family time.

Her solution? In addition to a generous array of medical, tuition, and retirement benefits, plus an annual $1,000 contribution to each employee's charity of choice through the company's Stellar Solutions Foundation, Ford invented what she calls an Individual Benefit Account (IBA). Following IRS regulations, Ford funds an account for each employee that can equal up to 25 percent of his base pay; how the money is spent depends on what each employee needs.

The most striking feature of the plan is how it provides equal compensation to each employee, along with the flexibility to spend it on what's most important to her: Employees with older parents, for instance, can designate money for elder care, whereas those with young children can choose child-friendly benefits. Ford is especially conscious of not offering employees "use it or lose it" vacation plans, a feature that she associates with her big-company experience. Employees can use their vacation time all at once, spread it out over the course of the year, or simply cash out the time.

Ford, like president and COO Colleen Barrett at Southwest Airlines, finds time to show a personal interest in each employee. On their first day at work, new employees receive a cookie bouquet from Ford and are treated to lunch with colleagues. They receive a card from Ford on each work anniversary, as well as on their birthday.

Ford doesn't neglect the financial side of the equation. In 2000, she launched Stellar Ventures, a venture capital fund for company spin-offs and related technology start-ups. The benefit for employees? They each have a stake in the fund, with the potential for bonuses based on how the new ventures perform. In the face of competition for talented employees from Silicon Valley start-ups, Ford offers her team the opportunity to get in on the ground floor of promising start-ups—without the risk of working for one.

How Can You Determine the Best Mix of Benefits for Your Employees?

In most companies, benefits are developed without keeping the varied needs of employees top of mind. And yet, no company can afford to give employees all the benefits they might like to have. So how can you develop the right mix—one that satisfies your employees and keeps your budget intact?

Our technique is based on research and dialogue. In a small company, you can talk to each individual. In a larger company, you can divide employees by segment, just as you would customers, using demographics, such as age, income, and family responsibilities, and psychographics, such as work/life balance needs. Using this information, you can set the stage for creating a portfolio that allows every employee to feel equally compensated.

Three Steps to Developing Benefits Options by Employee Segment

1. Determine the personal needs of each individual (or segment). How would this person define a win-win situation? Flex your own imagination and creativity to develop workable options.
2. Test your assumptions. Talk to each individual or representatives of each segment. Listen to what they need, both tangibly and emotionally. Ask them what they want—while cautioning them that you are there to listen, but that the final plan may not conform to any one person's wish list.
3. Compare their answers and feelings with yours. Develop benefits that are mutually satisfactory for both the employee and the company.

Stellar Solutions has succeeded in earning its employees' loyalty: Many of the people who joined Ford at the beginning are still with her. With all of this emphasis on its employees, however, how is Stellar Solutions performing? Approaching its tenth anniversary, the company is earning $10 million a year; in the past five years, it has grown an average of 15 percent per year.

And its clients? They include an impressive array of both government and private organizations, including the Central Intelligence Agency, the National Security Agency, the Department of Defense, NASA, IntelSat, DirecTV, Sirius CD Radio, Delta, and Lockheed. Both Lockheed and the CIA have cited the company for superior performance.

Stellar Solutions's brand statement is that the company satisfies its customers' critical needs; clearly, its strategy begins at home, satisfying the needs—and earning the loyalty—of its employees.

Now that we've seen how vital the CEO is in developing and maintaining employee loyalty on a day-to-day basis, how much more important is that leadership in times of change?

Let's find out.

15

Loyalty and Change Management

"It is not the strongest of the species that survive, nor the most intelligent, but the one most responsive to change."

—CHARLES DARWIN

Change is a proving ground, a test of what our true skills are as managers, leaders, and human beings. How do you handle adversity? Tragedy? Triumph? Uncertainty? As a company leader, the pressure is on you to do what's "best," leading your organization through periods of change in the way that will leave the company strongest, or, at least, least bruised.

Of course, businesses undergo a constant process of change and renewal: Employees get hired, trained, and moved through or out of the organization; customers are prospected, acquired, retained, lost, and won back; systems, technology, and physical plants need repairs, updates, and overhauls; new systems and facilities need to be built.

Times of major change, whether driven by a merger, an acquisition, a quarterly financial goal, competitive actions, or government regulations, are also times of stress. When companies deal with large-scale changes, employee loyalty can make or break a successful transition.

"The first responsibility of a leader is to define reality."

—MAX DE PREE, *LEADERSHIP IS AN ART*

In contrast to the empowerment that we discussed in Chapter 14, change is disempowering for those who are not in charge; as a result, change can trigger feelings of fear, stress, or even apathy among employees, lowering both their motivation to produce and their feelings of engagement with the organization.

Alan Rowe, author of *Creative Intelligence, Leadership, and the Challenge of the Future*, writes, "When a major adjustment is required . . . it can lead to high levels of 'fight, flight, or freeze.'" But is managing employees' feelings really part of a leader's job?[1]

In its 2004 report "An Overall Approach to Change Management," consulting firm Booz Allen Hamilton deals with this dilemma head-on. As the report states, "Business executives preparing their organizations for fundamental change generally struggle with accurately factoring human nature into the change equation. If management can . . . alleviate the inevitable human fear, anxiety, and discouragement during the transition, then the chances of implementing successful change will be greatly increased."[2]

As Booz Allen's report aptly illustrates, Loyalty Factor leadership is primarily a human skill. It requires CEOs to develop an understanding of employees' feelings, engage the employees in a constructive dialogue, and work with them to implement the CEO's guiding vision for the organization.

Empowering Your Loyalty Lieutenants

> *"Even if he [the President] ignores the advice . . . an outside advisor . . . can give the President a different perspective on his own situation; they can be frank with him when White House aides are not."*
>
> —CLARK CLIFFORD, *COUNSEL TO THE PRESIDENT*

Of course, no CEO should go it alone. Creating the Loyalty Factor relies on painstaking, honest observation, and a willingness to be frank—even blunt—about issues affecting employee loyalty. So who belongs on your loyalty management team?

As Daniel Goleman, psychologist and author of the best-selling book *Emotional Intelligence,* observed in the *American Journalism Review,* "The higher you go in any organization, as a leader, the less information and feedback you get about how you're performing as a leader. Because people are afraid to tell you."[3]

So who can leaders turn to for the honest, no-holds-barred advice that they need? Frances Hesselbein, chairman of the board of governors of the Leader to Leader Institute and former chief executive of Girl Scouts of the USA, calls on CEOs to incorporate what she calls "dispersed leadership," creating a chain of leaders at every level throughout the organization.[4, 5]

Can leaders really delegate the business of loyalty to their team members? The answer is yes, as long as the lines of communication stay open.

Many leaders also find value in turning to outside consultants for perspective on the issues facing their companies. After analyzing executive teams at 150 companies around the world, author and consultant Saj-nicole A. Joni observed that executives tend to rely on three primary types of advisers: personal friends and, often, an inner circle at work; experts in specific subjects within their companies; and outside consultants. Which executives were most effective? Those who used all the resources available to them to develop a truly rounded picture of their business. And which CEOs tend to get themselves, and their companies, into unnecessary trouble? Typically, those who forget to ask for—and respond to—their internal and external panels of experts.[6]

A Question of Faith

"Effective leaders are willing to take risks, think outside the box, and recognize that empowerment provides a sense of ownership to stakeholders that helps to assure proposed changes will be accepted."

—ALAN ROWE, AUTHOR, *CREATIVE INTELLIGENCE, LEADERSHIP, AND THE CHALLENGE OF THE FUTURE*

How do you generate a billion dollars in savings over ten years? That was the problem that KeySpan Energy faced a few years ago after merging with New England–based Eastern Enterprises.[7]

KeySpan was still going through growing pains from a merger that had taken place only two years before, when KeySpan, the parent company of Brooklyn Union Gas, merged with elements of the Long Island Lighting Company. While the company was still struggling to blend the Brooklyn and Long Island organizations, acquiring Eastern presented new challenges. Complex utility regulations required KeySpan to commit to saving $1 billion over a ten-year period—$100 million each year for a decade.

The merger had made KeySpan a vitally important utility, with over twelve thousand employees providing natural gas or electric service to almost four million customers. But even for a $6 billion organization,[8] $100 million a year is a lot of money.

One of the areas where the company realized that it could cut costs substantially was IT, but that would require the Brooklyn and Long Island staffs to finally integrate—and overcome years of rivalry. CEO Bob Catell asked KeySpan's internal HR consultant, Kenny Moore, to help get the IT staff out of their Brooklyn and Long Island silos and start contributing to the change process.[9]

Moore is a man who knows a lot about change. A Catholic monk for fifteen years, Moore left the monastery for the business world. Two years after joining the HR department of Brooklyn Union Gas, however, Moore was diagnosed with incurable non-Hodgkin's lymphoma.

Eventually, Moore was able to return to work, this time as Bob Catell's employee liaison. By then, Brooklyn Union was about to become KeySpan Energy, and Moore took on the responsibility of preparing the company's workers for the coming change. With Catell's active, if sometimes skeptical, support, Moore was able to bring a new perspective to the company's evolution.

In an interview with Tom Peters, Moore observed that change is like a journey: You have to leave something behind before you can go on to something new. That's why change is so hard for so many of us: We know that we may have to give up old habits, cherished relationships, entrenched attitudes.[10]

The job of change managers, in Moore's view, is to help employees understand the nature of the journey they're on, acknowledge the loss they may be experiencing, and start to envision the future that lies ahead. What he does not believe in is issuing employees a set of cut-and-dried directives. As Moore told Peters, "Change is about invitation. And invitation gets its power from the right of refusal. It's about choice."

When it came time to assess how the company would save $100 million a year, Moore's idea was to invite five hundred IT employees to a daylong meeting. KeySpan management, understandably, showed some resistance. Wouldn't such a large gathering be chaotic? There was no planned agenda—how would the day be focused? Or would hundreds of employees sit passively for a full day, with no movement on the issue at hand?[11]

"If KeySpan has nothing more than compliant employees, we are dead in the water. We will not be effective. We will not be successful. What we need are committed employees."

—KENNY MOORE, KEYSPAN ENERGY

Moore, however, wanted to encourage employees not just to develop, but to own the ideas that would change the company. As he said in an interview with HR.com, "The traditional way to engage employees is passive. I think what employees are looking for is to be a part of the conversation in an active way. Not to be told what to do, but to contribute and make suggestions."

Was Moore's faith in KeySpan's employees justified? In a word, yes. As dozens of people contributed their thoughts and observations, a strategy for finding the savings that the company needed began to emerge. Even more important, as Moore pointed out, ownership of the change initiative had shifted from management to the employees who would be responsible for making it happen.

By 2003, that one-day meeting had had a wide-ranging series of effects. First and foremost, the group had met its cost-cutting objectives. As an added benefit, the employee initiative helped break down the wall between the Brooklyn and Long Island outposts and opened the door to better, more efficient relationships with customers.

In addition to streamlining internal IT processes, KeySpan's IT department introduced a consolidated Web site, allowing customers to explore every aspect of the company quickly and easily, as well as manage their accounts online. Since the Web site included more than fifteen hundred pages of both regulated and unregulated content, this was no easy feat, but the effort was rewarded, as the Loyalty Factor predicts, by both increased customer loyalty and increased brand loyalty.

Customer use of the new and improved company Web site—
now with an interactive customer service interface, a streamlined,
brand-conscious look, and comprehensive, timely information—
increased by 300 percent. Revenues rose as a result of online sales
of products and services, and the efficiency of customer service
and transactions increased.[12]

As a result of these and other initiatives spearheaded by
Moore, KeySpan has become an industry leader in providing customer service and creating customer satisfaction. In 2004, KeySpan
Corporation outranked every other gas utility in the American
Customer Satisfaction Index (ACSI), produced by the University
of Michigan Business School in partnership with the American
Society for Quality, and the consulting firm CFI Group. Although
the scores for U.S. utilities as a whole hadn't changed from the
past year, KeySpan's score had improved by over 4 percent.

KeySpan won another award in 2004, which helps illustrate its
success, as well as the close connection between customer loyalty
and brand loyalty. What did it win? The 2004 Customer Loyalty
Award from *Brandweek*, the magazine for managers of corporate
brands.[13]

In their book, *The CEO and the Monk*, Kenny Moore
and Bob Catell recount the experiences the two
shared in reinventing KeySpan's culture. One well-
known anecdote reflects Moore's idea that every
beginning must be preceded by an ending.

When it came time to prepare the company for the
transition from Brooklyn Union to KeySpan Energy,
Moore drew on his past experience to create a
change management event. With about sixty skeptical, puzzled, and in some cases irritated executives

gathered in a conference room, Moore stood next to a stand holding a large funeral wreath and, with Gregorian chants playing in the background, began the meeting with these words: "Dearly beloved, we are gathered here today to bid a fond farewell to the Brooklyn Union of the past."

Providing Permission to Change

"Leadership is everything. If you don't have the right people at the top, it is too difficult to accomplish—and sustain—either the business mission or the supporting people mission."

—VICTORIA BERGER-GROSS, TIFFANY & CO.

Even companies experiencing normal growing pains need to evaluate their change management skills and leadership initiatives. At New York City–based Tiffany & Co., CEO Michael J. Kowalski brought in help—not to change the venerable company, but to give it new energy.

When Tiffany & Co. opened its doors for business back in 1837, it had two employees and first-day sales of $4.98.[14] Today, with its flagship store on Fifth Avenue, in the heart of New York City, Tiffany & Co. employs almost seven thousand people around the world and sells over $2 billion in merchandise every year.[15]

The company has changed in other ways as well. It has vertically integrated many of its procedures, employing not only the gracious clerks and gift wrappers at its retail stores, but diamond cutters, designers, and manufacturers in such disparate locations as Yellowknife, Canada, and Antwerp, Belgium.[16]

Historically, Tiffany's employee loyalty has been exemplary: A number of workers have been with the company for decades, and annual turnover has been about 9 percent—half the national average. As the company grew, however, management sensed a need to strengthen its ties with employees, both new and old, in order to maintain the legacy of loyalty through the period of widespread changes in the organization.

In early 2001, the company hired Dr. Victoria Berger-Gross as senior vice president of human resources. Her mission? To maintain and manage the company's entrenched culture.[17]

As Berger-Gross began to observe and evaluate the culture, however, she noticed certain disconnects. For instance, communication between senior and midlevel management was repressed. The internal culture combined tremendous respect for authority with a desire for avoiding conflict—up to the point where vice presidents refused to offer even constructive criticism without permission.

What was Berger-Gross's solution? With the blessing of CEO Kowalski, President Jim Quinn, and the rest of the senior management team, she developed a series of discussions designed to develop leadership skills among the company's vice presidents. The forums were an opportunity to raise the issues that had traditionally been avoided—or not even considered.[18]

One of the first questions Berger-Gross asked was: What's working—and what isn't? The chief asset that employees identified was a two-edged sword: The strong internal community created a family-like atmosphere, but managers and employees had a difficult time discussing issues that came up in the workplace. Keeping the peace and avoiding conflict between colleagues had become more important than ironing out performance problems.

The forums proved to be the energizing lift that the company needed. The vice presidents left the training sessions with new insights on how to manage their staff relationships. With the help of

Berger-Gross's HR staff, the executives developed the company's first-ever employee evaluation process.

With her years of experience, Berger-Gross could no doubt have created and implemented an evaluation system without investing time and effort in training sessions. However, her process allowed the idea to grow organically from the very people who would need to implement it. As a result, the delicate fabric of Tiffany's historic culture was reshaped without being torn.

And how did those reporting to the VP level react? Surprisingly, perhaps, a large proportion of Tiffany's managers and frontline workers greeted the changes with a sigh of relief. Having operated for so long without feedback, many workers saw the evaluation process as an opportunity to learn how they could improve their performance. And since the evaluations were implemented across the board, the process was objective; no one employee had to face the embarrassment of being singled out for praise or blame.

Tiffany & Co. has continued to engage its employees in an active dialogue, and to listen to, and act on, the results.

Developing the Dialogue in Your Company

How can you develop the teamwork and dedication to change that KeySpan and Tiffany created among their employees? Here is our simple step-by-step technique for conducting a brainstorming session that produces results:

1. Begin with a goal: What's the business objective you hope to achieve with this brainstorming meeting?

2. Write down the key question you want to answer or the key issue you want to discuss, such as, "How can we consolidate our operations?" or "Now that the structure of our organization has evolved, how can our culture evolve in a positive way?"

Write down your own answers to the questions as a guideline. At this point, you may also find that you want to refine the way you describe the central issue under discussion.

3. Call a staff meeting, preferably from 9:00 to 12:00, when people are fresh. Ask people to turn off their cell phones and pagers; provide light refreshments and writing materials at each seat. Make sure that the room has a whiteboard and/or an easel and plenty of working markers.

4. Begin by explaining the purpose of the meeting and what you expect to achieve with the participants' help. Tell the group members that they're your "brain trust" for this problem, and remind them that creativity is welcome. The only rule is not to edit or negate others' ideas.

5. Pose your question and record answers on the flip chart or whiteboard.

6. If the brainstorming slows down, ask questions to prompt answers. If you still have items on your own list that haven't come up, go ahead and contribute them yourself.

You'll probably see head nods and other signs of agreement regarding your suggestions.

7. When you have a number of suggestions, invite everyone to take a few minutes to jot down what they think are the five best responses to the problem. You can also invite them to add any thoughts of their own that they may not have voiced yet.

8. Once everyone has written her selections, divide the group members into clusters of three and ask the people in each cluster to compare notes. Their goal? To reduce the list of fifteen or so answers to three or four of the strongest and actionable. This part of the session should not be longer than fifteen minutes.

9. At the end of fifteen minutes, ask each group to read its answers out loud. Go back to where you've recorded the brainstorming ideas and circle items as they come up. If there are twenty people in the room, you should now have a list of about twenty to thirty items (most likely including some duplicates).

10. Quickly run down the list of items, asking the group to categorize each item by priority (A, B, or C); the majority rules. You'll finish the exercise with three groups of initiatives, each labeled as top, medium, or low priority. Ask the group to look at the top-priority list one last time. Do the choices make sense? Do any issues come to mind?

11. Once everyone feels satisfied with the list of top priorities, the meeting is over. Explain the next steps, which will include a memo confirming the final list of priorities, and a request for each participant to volunteer to lead one of the initiatives.

12. Close the session with thanks for the group's enthusiasm and creativity. Thank everyone for the contribution they're making to the corporate culture and the company's healthy growth.

So who gets credit for the smooth evolution of Tiffany's corporate culture? CEO Kowalski and President Quinn played perhaps the most vital roles: Without their active interest and understanding of the issues, the project would never have gotten under way.

As management's designated leader, Dr. Berger-Gross was able to implement a program to develop changes based on employees' concerns and help those same employees develop action plans to implement their ideas.

Last but not least, empowered middle managers were able to explain the changes to their staffs. Their belief in and enthusiasm for the program created an atmosphere of acceptance, rather than resentment—not a bad achievement for implementing major change in a culture almost two hundred years old.

Change in business is inevitable. So, unfortunately, is crisis—a period of heightened, intense change. How can the Loyalty Factor prepare you and your company to manage disruptions, both large and small? Let's look at what some companies have done to plan for, and to manage, real-life disasters.

16

Loyalty in Times of Crisis

Question: "Mr. Secretary, what are you advising the people
who work at these businesses to do? Tomorrow's a
workday; should they go to work, should they stay away?"
Secretary Ridge: "We have talked to the security
professionals at those buildings and the leadership, and I
think the employees most appropriately would get
guidance from their employer."[1]

—SECRETARY OF HOMELAND SECURITY TOM RIDGE

We live in an era in which crisis—from natural disasters to
cyberterrorism—has to be factored into any company's
contingency plans. Managers who need to rally the troops in times
of crisis need a swift, effective, action-oriented process that is spe-
cifically geared toward managing heightened periods of tension
within the organization.

Our five-step Crisis Management process (a short-term variant on the Loyalty Factor process) provides a plan of action that any manager can use to lead successfully in times of crisis or heightened change:

1. Listen to and engage employees, customers, and business partners *before* a crisis happens to understand potential issues and develop strategies for business continuity.

2. Develop a top-line plan to create solutions for potential problems.

3. Nominate change agents to develop tactical implementation plans; train front-line managers in the skills necessary to implement the required procedures.

4. Communicate crisis procedures to the entire organization to address fears and develop support.

5. Run virtual "fire drills"; update procedures annually.

Will Crisis Affect Your Company?

"Most of the direct victims of terrorism in the United States in recent years have been people at work."[2]

—CONGRESSIONAL RESEARCH SERVICE, "TERRORISM: THE NEW
OCCUPATIONAL HAZARD"

We live in an era of constant threats to business: deliberate, accidental, and natural. How well are your employees prepared to cope with the stress of unexpected events and the resulting disruption? How much have you done to protect them in the event of a problem? Thinking about these issues in advance not only will help your company create a vital preparedness strategy, but will signal to your employees that you care about their very survival.

In the event that your company does experience a serious problem, your employees will be armed with the knowledge that

they need in order to function effectively, calmly, and purpose-
fully, preserving critical business information to the extent possible and keeping the various parts of the organization in touch.

Of course, all of us are conscious of the potential impact of
terrorism. While terrorism may not be an everyday threat for most
U.S. companies, it's an ever-present one. According to the U.S.
Department of State, in every year between 1998 and 2002, businesses around the world were terrorist targets more often than
diplomatic, government, or military facilities.[3] These figures include, of course, the horrific events of September 11, 2001, the
most dramatic example the world has ever seen of the destruction
of what were primarily workplaces for thousands of people.

And although the United States has not been subjected to a
drumbeat of terrorist acts, other countries have not been so fortu-
nate: So many businesses operating in Latin America are at risk of
having executives and their family members kidnapped, for instance, that insurance companies now offer coverage against such
incidents.

Warnings alone can create a serious disruption. On Sunday,
August 1, 2004, acting on information from the federal government, the New York Police Department alerted a number of specific companies of possible threats involving car or truck bombs,
as well as chemical agents.[4] Similar threats were active in Washington, D.C. and New Jersey.

The following morning, Citigroup's midtown Manhattan
headquarters, one of the possible targets, was surrounded by police
patrols, bomb-sniffing dogs—and an army of news reporters vying
for space in front of the entrances. Employees arriving for work
had to navigate this gauntlet just to approach the building; before
entering, they waited in line to be cleared through a security check-
point.[5]

Just a few days later, Hurricane Charley made landfall in Florida; at this writing, economists estimate that the storm's 145-mile-
an-hour winds could have caused more than $11 billion in per-
sonal and business loss and cost the lives of twenty-five people.[6]

Different parts of the country have to cope with fires, floods, landslides, blizzards, and other natural disasters, forcing businesses in those areas to function with fewer employees than usual, or with employees who are worried about picking up their children, connecting with their spouses, protecting their homes, or just commuting to or from work.

And every day, more mundane incidents, from water main breaks to gas line leaks to power outages, can disrupt business for hours or days.

The cultures of organizations are most often revealed, and sometimes strengthened, in times of crisis. Loyalties can be quickly cemented or destroyed, depending on how individuals and organizations behave. So how can company leaders plan for, and respond to, disasters in ways that will cement employee loyalty and win the loyalty and admiration of customers and other stakeholders?

Bob Davis Is Dead

"Before 9/11, if you conducted a fire drill, people ignored it. But now . . . it's a valued exercise—something that their employer is doing to protect them."

—WENDI STRONG, EXECUTIVE VICE PRESIDENT OF CORPORATE
COMMUNICATIONS, USAA

At 10:30 on a Wednesday morning in July, it was confirmed that Bob Davis, chairman and CEO of USAA, one of the country's largest diversified financial services companies, was dead. This was one of a chain of horrifying events that had begun early that same day, including a bomb exploding in the company's San Antonio, Texas, headquarters; an anthrax attack; a widespread outbreak of severe food poisoning; and the threat of a category-4 hurricane.[7]

Thousands of USAA's employees were evacuated from five million square feet of office space on its 286-acre campus. The

Texas state insurance commissioner was notified; the San Antonio fire department and EMTs helped guide employees to safety and provided medical care. Local news media came to the scene with cameras ready to roll.

Actually, it was all a drill, designed to test USAA's disaster preparedness strategy. Nobody died. The objective was to teach USAA's employees—from the most senior executives to the most junior staff members—how to handle disasters that could affect everything from their ability to do business to their personal safety.

The dramatic and realistic scenario raised issues even greater than the challenge of moving thousands of people from point A to point B: The company made a great effort to understand and help employees manage their reactions in a time of crisis—emotions that could conceivably range from fear to panic to stubborn refusal to leave the office. In addition, the company needed to understand how it would continue managing its members' transactions in the event of a major disaster.

The cornerstone of the plan was communication. USAA's strategy covered what to say, and to whom, as well as how to communicate messages that would keep the business functioning while employees were rescued and/or evacuated. The company included situations in its drill that required everything from personal relays from department managers to top executives, to creating press releases and dealing with on-site news reporters. It experimented with a wide range of communication techniques to test the effectiveness of everything from cell phones and walkie-talkies to the company intercom system.

Protecting against disaster is actually part of USAA's core business, as a major provider of insurance and financial services. By showing employees how carefully the company was planning for their safety, it demonstrated the company's loyalty to the people it counts on to make its business succeed.

USAA's disaster management plan is only one element of a comprehensive program designed to foster loyalty among its

21,000 employees. The company is cited by numerous sources—including *Working Mother, Computerworld, Latina Style,* and *G.I. Jobs*—as being one of the best places to work in the country.[8]

And how do customers react? One answer comes from a 2004 Forrester Research survey, which named USAA the No. 1 financial services company for customer advocacy. Eighty-two percent of the USAA members surveyed by Forrester said they trusted the company to act in their best interests. The No. 2 company scored only 62 percent among its own customers. Of the 6,000 people surveyed, 67 percent said that they would consider USAA for their next insurance purchase—only one of the other companies in the survey even exceeded 50 percent.

What's the single greatest criterion for being named a customer advocate? According to Forrester, it's putting customers' needs first in the minds of employees in every department, at every level. Clearly, USAA extends that principle to its employees as well. With sales of over $10 billion, and steady year-over-year increases,[9] USAA proves that loyal employees create loyal customers—and improve the value of the brand.

Diagnosing your employees' needs in advance of a problem is an extraordinarily valuable tool for ensuring your employees' safety and peace of mind—as well as for developing their loyalty. A real crisis, however, provides its own unique test of management's leadership abilities and employees' dedication to the organization.

A Matter of Life or Death

"You don't know the details you're missing . . . until you're dealing with a disaster."

—JOHN HALAMKA, BIDMC

Beth Israel Deaconess Medical Center (BIDMC) is one of Boston's best-known and most-respected medical facilities, combining patient care, teaching, and research in affiliation with Harvard Medical School.

On November 13, 2002, BIDMC CIO John Halamka noticed that his computer was taking an unusually long time to process e-mail. It was around 1:45 P.M. Fifteen minutes later, the entire system—called the nation's best in health care just one year earlier by *Information Week*—crashed. With an active emergency room and patients occupying 85 percent of the hospital's beds, the meltdown could have meant disaster for BIDMC, where access to information literally saves lives.[10]

Like most organizations, BIDMC depends on a constant stream of e-mails and electronic data capture and reporting. Without the online systems, doctors couldn't access medical records; the pharmacy couldn't fill patient prescriptions. Billing couldn't be processed, including insurance and Medicare information.

How did the hospital handle the crisis? As CIO, Halamka took the lead in getting the system restored—and in keeping the entire staff focused. What was his secret? Operating on almost no sleep for several days, Halamka remembered his experience years before, when he was training in the emergency room of LA's Harbor-UCLA Medical Center during a period of intense gang violence. His first rule then—and now: Be calm; be friendly.

BIDMC's staff in every department took their cue from Halamka. Rather than transfer vulnerable patients, hospital employees from CEO Paul Levy on down worked overtime to keep vital services running. Doctors manned copiers; microbiologists picked up results from the lab. In all, hundreds of employees, from lab technicians to Harvard-trained cardiac fellows, mobilized to physically transfer 250,000 sheets of paper containing vital patient information (everything that was normally circulated electronically) from one end of the main hospital campus to the other.[11]

There were some unexpected benefits. Employees from every department, at every level of the hospital hierarchy, suddenly needed to work with others face-to-face. With John Halamka's example of staying calm and friendly, lines blurred between departments whose workers normally would never get to know each other.

The crisis also led to some unanticipated teamwork between Veteran and Boomer staff members and their younger Gen X and Nexter colleagues as those in the "IT generations" got a sudden introduction to a pre-IT environment. Younger staff members in particular had a hard time adjusting to the situation. Trained in practicing medicine with the assistance of a reliable, data-packed computer network, they now relied on their more experienced colleagues for help in handling the demands of patient care without their familiar tools. Young doctors, for instance, who were used to tapping prescriptions into a PDA and receiving instant feedback on drug interactions and other vital information, had to learn how to write a prescription on paper—and ask for help to confirm their memories of allergic reactions and dosages.

Stress levels were high, and more than one doctor was scared. Would they make mistakes? Would someone die? As the IT department worked around the clock and every employee of the hospital pitched in, patients were served. In fact, no one was reported hurt at any time during the disruption.

The crisis continued from Wednesday afternoon through Sunday night: Halamka's team had the hospital's system up and running again by early Monday morning. What had the problem been? Something that in our day and age could affect virtually any company at any time: a new type of computer virus that spread uncontrollably throughout the network.

Was BIDMC's Experience Unusual?

Research indicates that an average technology-based disruption lasts about eighteen hours, although 20 percent of system failures last forty-eight hours or more. Disruptions affect staff productivity about two-thirds of the time, resulting in anything from inconvenience to catastrophe. Half of the disruptions that businesses experience also result in a serious or catastrophic loss of revenue and/or customers.

BIDMC's problem was not the result of a malicious act. But what about cybercrime? The 2004 E-Crime Watch survey, conducted by *CSO* magazine in cooperation with the U.S. Secret Service and the Carnegie Mellon University Software Engineering Institute's CERT Coordination Center, reports that 70 percent of organizations have experienced at least one e-crime in the past year, and 43 percent say that such crimes are increasing. The cost of cybercrime? In 2003 alone, reported crimes cost approximately $666 million.[12]

What happened after the network came back on? As one of the country's foremost medical centers, BIDMC's staff members could have relied on their stature to continue doing "business as usual." Instead, they treated the challenge they had undergone together as an opportunity to improve their commitment to patient health and safety even further.

John Halamka reviewed the technology behind BIDMC's applications, improving the system so that it would be a model for care centers around the country. With the support of CEO Levy, Halamka has kept the memory of the problem active, using it as a teaching tool within the BIDMC organization, as well as for other computer-reliant organizations throughout the country.[13]

The lessons learned at BIDMC went much further than system development. In August 2004, a national study by the Economic and Social Research Institute named BIDMC as a top performer in improving health and safety, citing BIDMC for its commitment to change and its empowerment of its physicians, nurses, pharmacists, and other staff members to identify, examine, and improve problem areas.[14]

The lesson is revealing: Even as technology continues to supplement our skills and knowledge, we're still innately dependent on the minds and bodies of the people who work with us. As the old saying goes, your most important company assets take the elevator down every night. They're the reason your organization works.

The Loyalty Factor Foundation

"Every day that a business is closed is a day of lost revenue—and one step closer to the doors closing permanently."

—JOHN COPENHAVER, CHAIRMAN OF THE BOARD, GLOBAL PARTNERSHIP
FOR PREPAREDNESS

How much can disaster affect your organization? Larger companies tend to experience, at a minimum, a loss of productivity and revenue. For the 99 percent of companies in the United States with five hundred employees or fewer, the results might be more drastic. According to statistics from a University of Texas study, if small businesses are forced to close, 43 percent of them never reopen, 51 percent close permanently after two years, and only 6 percent survive longer than that.

It's a complicated world, but there's one simple question that must be answered: Are you—and your employees—prepared?

How would you manage your business if your building or factory or computers or phones weren't available—for a day, a week, a month? Building the Loyalty Factor into your company's everyday management will help your company, and you, bridge periods of crisis.

When company leaders incorporate the principles of the Loyalty Factor, they develop what author and management consultant Daniel Goleman calls "emotional capital": the positive feelings that a leader can draw on in low periods, and particularly in times of crisis.[15]

In their book *The Courage to Act*, Merom Klein and Rod Napier remind us that in the heat of a crisis, leaders and organizations need courage—a quality reflected by what you do when you are put to the test and face moments of truth. How do they define the key elements of courage? The authors cite candor, purpose, will, rigor, and risk.

For leaders managing in times of change or crisis—that is, all of us—these traits can be transformed into five specific strategies:

1. To speak and hear the truth—even if it's unpleasant or painful

2. To concentrate on the big picture, giving employees the opportunity to identify specific strategies and tactics to achieve it

3. To inspire confidence in the company and its mission, and pride among employees

4. To recognize how your own actions affect everyone—for better or worse

5. And finally, and in our view most crucial, to empower, trust, and invest in relationships

As the Marines would say, *semper fi.*

17

Some of Our Favorite Stories:
The Loyalty Factor at Work

"You've got to give loyalty down, if you want loyalty up."

—DONALD T. REGAN

Companies that embody the values of the Loyalty Factor, like those we've looked at throughout this book, understand that quality of life affects quality of work. They know that employees' satisfaction, empowerment, and sense of belonging have a direct impact on how they do their jobs and the quality that they imbue in every action, from answering the phone to writing a spreadsheet, from manning a manufacturing station to packing and shipping product.

Customers know quality when they see it, and they tend to

come back for more. Their satisfaction translates into your company's revenues. As customers spread the word about your products and services, and analysts notice your company's profits and productivity, your company becomes a true brand: a name that instantly stands for a set of values, product quality, and unparalleled service.

I couldn't resist telling just a few more stories about companies that I think embody the principles and values of the Loyalty Factor. I think that these stories, like the stories I've been telling throughout the book, can add some ideas to your repertoire for creating the Loyalty Factor in your place of business.

Leadership at Every Level

"Knowledge is most valuable when it is controlled and used by those on the front lines of the organization."[1]

—C. A. Bartlett and S. Ghoshal, *Harvard Business Review*

What kind of company has seven hundred bosses? For one, California's Graniterock, a century-old heavy engineering contractor. When *Fortune Small Business* listed Graniterock in its 2003 "Best Bosses" issue, it honored the employees as a group.[2]

In fact, when Graniterock's team filled out the award's application form to have the company considered, it didn't single out president and CEO Bruce W. Woolpert. Instead, it had the unique idea of declaring that all of Graniterock's employees met the "bosses' standard" defined by *Fortune* and its survey partner, Winning Workplaces. The innovative approach alone caught *Fortune's* eye: Graniterock was the only company to take the approach that all of its employees were leaders—responsible for making decisions as well as getting results.

Graniterock does not claim to be a glamorous business. As

Nancy K. Austin described the company in *Inc.* magazine, it is "in the ancient and unimaginably gritty business of quarrying and crushing rock."[3]

The company expects its employees to be aware of the company's performance goals and to take personal responsibility for improving both their own and their team's efficiency practices. But CEO Woolpert knows that it's management's responsibility to create an environment in which this can happen.

Woolpert explains the company's management philosophy this way: "The role of a manager is not to direct people's activity, but . . . to support the learning and skill development of others so each person can lead his or her own work. This gives each team member unusual control and authority to direct how his or her work gets done and how it is improved. At Graniterock, we call this self-leadership."

Graniterock clearly understands that employees are the key to customer loyalty. As it explains on its Web site, "Graniterock's Corporate Objectives and Values . . . [make] it easier to attract and keep the best people in the industry. . . . And that's how we deliver the value, quality, and service you and the rest of the industry have come to expect."[4]

The company stresses high quality in its materials, processes, service, and delivery, a prime differentiator in an industry that is sometimes criticized for providing substandard materials and service. Graniterock's revolutionary idea? To do things right the first time.

Part of its strategy is a strong emphasis on training. On average, employees receive about forty hours of training each year; the company invests in training three times more than the average mining company and thirteen times more than the average construction company.[5]

Graniterock's training programs range from teaching employees how to operate the company's fleet of construction vehicles to highly technical skills such as statistical process control. The company offers employees seminars on quality management and invites outside speakers to give talks on such topics as teamwork and quality improvement.

One result? According to industry journal *Masonry*, the company's productivity, defined as revenue earned per employee, is about 30 percent higher than the national industry average.

And that's not the only way in which Graniterock outpaces its peers. Customers are reliably happy with the company's work. While Graniterock offers a money-back guarantee, its cost to resolve customer complaints is only about 0.2 percent of sales—one-tenth the industry average.

Is there any downside to the company? We found one: The company's profile on the Web site for *Graduating Engineer*, a magazine for newly minted engineering and technical professionals, says that the biggest problem with the company is that "it's hard to get in. Few people leave unless they retire."[6]

Setting the Course: A Lesson in Leadership

> *"Hiring, training, motivating, compensating, and retaining talented employees have become as essential as building factories and purchasing machinery were during the Industrial Age. More than ever, a committed, engaged work force generates value for the company and loyalty among customers, which partly explains the fierce competition for top talent."*[7]
>
> —BOB WOODS, "HARVESTING YOUR HUMAN CAPITAL," CHIEF EXECUTIVE

When CEO Kevin Sharer joined Amgen (the largest biotechnology company on the face of the earth) after an executive career with GE and MCI, he was sure of his management skills, but he recognized that biotech was not his strong suit. Although Sharer holds multiple graduate degrees and has an undergraduate degree from the U.S. Naval Academy at Annapolis, his education in pure science prior to joining Amgen was limited to high school biology and college chemistry.

So as his career path at Amgen moved steadily toward the CEO's office, Sharer decided to get back to the business of learning. His goal? In order to be able to have the kind of conversations that would move the company ahead with stakeholders in every area, Sharer determined to learn everything he could about Amgen's core functions (scientific research and development) and about managing the diverse array of scientists, pharmacists, salespeople, manufacturers, and other stakeholders that are key to Amgen's success.

As Sharer described his self-directed training to Charles Fishman in *Fast Company*, "For probably a year and a half, I was a steady student.[8] I read textbooks and I spent a lot of time in the laboratories of our top people here. I hired my old firm—McKinsey & Co.—to be my tutor in pharmaceuticals and biotechnology."

Sharer educated himself on another key factor as well: what his employees wanted, needed, and were most anxious about concerning the change in leadership.

What was his first step? Asking questions—and listening to the answers. Before he was appointed CEO, Sharer asked each of his top managers to answer five questions, which, according to one account, were the following:[9]

1. What three things do you want to change?

2. What three things do you want to keep?

3. What are you most worried I might do?

4. What do you want me to do?

5. Is there anything else you want to talk about?

Sharer spoke to each executive personally, tabulated the results of their answers—and shared his findings with the company. It was that in-depth learning about the people responsible for managing Amgen that gave Sharer the information he needed to run the company effectively.

How has Sharer's education affected his company? Listed as one of the Fortune 500, Forbes 500, and *Financial Times* Global 500, Amgen has also been named one of *Barron's* top investment performers among the largest U.S. and Canadian companies.[10]

Knowing that career development is a key concern of employees in his industry, Sharer believes in educating employees as well.[11] In addition to offering employees up to forty hours of professional development each year, the company's benefits package includes $10,000 in tuition reimbursement.

Amgen even takes its passion for learning into the community. Each year, the company presents the Amgen Award for Science Teaching Excellence to a select group of science teachers in grades K through 12 who show both a commitment to and a talent for teaching science to young people.[12]

Employees—and prospective hires—see the value Amgen offers them. According to *Fortune*, Amgen receives over 120,000 job applications each year, but with only 8 percent turnover, new hires are mostly brought into jobs created by company growth.

Those new hires are the result of new sales—a good indicator of customer satisfaction. In 2004, *Business 2.0* named Amgen one of the 100 fastest-growing technology companies of the year. And although the company's stock has lagged while Wall Street looks for even more evidence of innovation, the company's $8.4 billion in sales in 2003, as *Business Week* noted, "dwarfed those of its nearest competitors."[13]

Bringing Out the Best in People

It's one of our favorite outcomes of the Loyalty Factor: When you give your employees the opportunity to do and be their best, most of the time they will exceed even your highest expectations.

As a leader, you have the ability to give employees the freedom and encouragement to do their best by helping them to

- Discover skills and capacity that they may not have even known they had.
- Develop and learn new skills.
- Find opportunities to make meaningful contributions: to the company, the community, and society at large.

And how do you do that? As we tell our clients, there are only three simple rules to keep in mind:

1. Ask questions—and respect the answers.
2. Be enthusiastic, upbeat, and positive about the employee's current and potential contributions to the company.
3. Reframe goals and objectives to encourage new levels of performance and commitment.

Doing Well by Doing Good

"Contrary to the cliché, genuinely nice guys most often finish first, or very near it."

—MALCOLM S. FORBES

"Act as if the whole world were watching."

—THOMAS JEFFERSON

Jeff Swartz's grandfather Nathan built boots. And although he most likely didn't anticipate the language of corporate America and the idea of corporate social responsibility (CSR), he taught his children and grandchildren how to run an honorable business and live an honorable life.

Swartz is the CEO of The Timberland Company, the third generation to run the company that his grandfather founded. Swartz is also a leader in corporate responsibility, committed to both doing well and doing good.

In addition to making and selling its signature boot and other outdoor gear, Timberland has committed itself to community service—and as a global company, Timberland takes a wide view of its community.

One of the company's first community service acts began relatively close to home. In 1989, a Boston-based nonprofit organization called City Year sent Timberland, located in nearby New Hampshire, a request to donate boots. City Year, an "urban Peace Corps," enlists young people from different backgrounds to serve their communities for a year. As Swartz recalled in an article for *Brookings Review*, "The letter described 50 young people, out to save the world, lacking only boots for their feet. Would I send along the boots?"[14]

Swartz had received many such requests before, but this one struck him in a new way. Not only did he send the boots, he accepted a challenge from City Year cofounder Alan Khazei to spend four hours working with him and a small group of young City Year volunteers.

Swartz didn't have to go far—City Year had a project just a mile from Timberland's headquarters. How did he help save the world? He painted some walls—in a group home for young, recovering addicts.

Timberland has remained an active partner with City Year from that day to this. His own experience inspired Swartz to create opportunities for Timberland employees to volunteer. In 1992, Timberland introduced a program called "the Path of Service," giving Timberland employees forty hours of paid time every year for volunteer work in their communities. In the years since, according to Timberland, its employees "have served more than 250,000 community service hours, helping to strengthen hundreds of communities across the world."

If there's one event that exemplifies Timberland's community service ideals, it's the company's annual one-day global Serv-a-palooza. For twenty-four hours, the doors of every Timberland outpost everywhere in the world are shut, and employees join with business partners and consumers to participate in local community service initiatives.

In 2003, the company reported that 4,500 Timberland employees, business partners, and consumers provided "the equivalent of more than 3.5 years of 24-hours-a-day, seven-days-a-week community service in a single day."[15] The event's projects included beautifying a Philadelphia youth center, upgrading community parks in Malaysia, renovating school libraries and classrooms in South Africa, and restoring the grounds of a home for the aged in the United Kingdom.

Timberland finds that providing the opportunity to serve is an attraction for new hires. Research indicates that companies with strong social responsibility programs find it easier to recruit employees, particularly in tight labor markets and, significantly, among Gen Xers. One survey suggested that about half of Gen Xers would even accept a lower salary in order to work for a socially responsible company.[16]

The company's philosophy of social responsibility also creates strong loyalty among its current staff. Volunteering on "Timberland time" gives employees a strong sense of pride in their company and themselves; in fact, some employees are motivated to volunteer additional personal time to the organizations they care about, thanks to the start they got from Timberland.

In a recent employee survey, 91 percent of the respondents ranked paid time off for community service as one of the company benefits that they value most. Industry studies suggest that they are not unique: Organizations that recognize the deeper meanings in life tend to have higher morale; more motivated, innovative employees; and higher levels of employee satisfaction and productivity.[17]

As a leader who makes community service a priority, Jeff Swartz also gets high marks from his company on personal integrity.

A global study by Walker Information Global Network and the Hudson Institute says that a leader's integrity is another key driver of employee loyalty. Employees who believe that their company leaders have, and demonstrate, a high level of personal integrity are far more likely to have a deep sense of loyalty to their companies than those workers who believe that their leaders are less ethical. According to the Society of Human Resource Management, "An ethical and honest culture can bolster employee morale and ultimately increase shareholder value. Employees who perceive that their leaders are ethical have a greater level of job satisfaction and feel more valued as workers."[18]

A culture of community service can also be a strong marketing tool: As customers evaluate their choices for the products and services they want to buy, they tend to prefer working with companies whose values they respect. In the case of companies like Timberland, which offer hands-on community service close to home, loyalty is created in the hearts and minds of neighbors and local governments, leading to greater support for the company's products, people, and future plans.

In terms of business analysis, what does all this community service do for company profits? Plenty. In August 2004, *Industry Week* named Timberland one of its "50 Best-Managed Manufacturing Companies."[19] The criteria? The winners were judged on revenue growth, profit margin, inventory turns, asset turnover, return on assets, and return on equity.

Since Timberland took on its first large-scale community service project with City Year back in 1989, revenues have grown from $156 million to $1.3 billion in 2003.[20] As Jeff Swartz has said, "A strong commitment to volunteering and civic responsibility serves corporate interests as well as community, national, and global needs by increasing employee productivity and employee, consumer, and shareholder loyalty."

It's the Loyalty Factor at work.

Afterword

We've been developing and teaching the principles of the Loyalty Factor for years. Time after time, we've seen the power of our formula in businesses of every description: *Employee loyalty leads to customer loyalty, which drives brand loyalty.*

As we hope you've seen, the Loyalty Factor can be developed, and take hold, in companies large and small, in any industry, and at any level of the organization, from CEOs to call center workers.

If one ingredient is crucial to the success of the Loyalty Factor, however, it's leadership. Creating the Loyalty Factor requires a leader with a strong commitment to his or her company's success and a fundamental belief in the energy and talents of the people who show up for work every day. Loyalty Factor leaders know that customer loyalty, brand loyalty, and the loyalty of the whole constellation of stakeholders starts at home, with the people who make the organization's brand promise a reality.

And while creating and implementing the Loyalty Factor can start with specific business functions, everyone who touches any aspect of your business is a candidate for the Loyalty Factor. Why? Because each person has a role to play in the quality of your product or service, and ultimately in your customer's experience with what he or she buys from your company.

The economic challenges for business in the years ahead will be best met with a strong, loyal workforce, with employees who are empowered to achieve their personal ambitions while creating company growth.

This book is intended as an invitation for you to bring the Loyalty Advantage into your company, and into the lives of the people who work with you and for you.

I hope you find the rewards as compelling, and as gratifying, as we do.

References

Chapter 1

1. The Marine Corps Motto, *Customs and Traditions*, U.S. Marine Corps, History and Museum Division, www.usmc.mil.

2. Robert East, Julie Sinclair, and Phil Gendall, "Loyalty: Definition and Explanation," ANZMAC 2000, Visionary Marketing for the 21st Century, www/anzmac2000/cdsite/papers/e/east1.pdf.

3. *Webster's Ninth New Collegiate Dictionary* (Springfield, Mass.: Merriam-Webster, Inc., 1985), p. 708

4. Robert K. Barnhart, *Dictionary of Etymology* (Harperresource, 1995), p. 444.

5. Nancy DeWolf Smith, "A Trip Back in Time with Baggage," *Wall Street Journal*, May 14, 2004, p. W7.

6. Clayton Act, 15 U.S.C. § 17, Antitrust Division Manual, www.usdoj.gov.

7. Professor Theron Schlabach, "Rationality and Welfare: Public Discussion of Poverty and Social Insurance in the United States 1875–1935," Social Security Online, www.ssa.gov.

8. Ricco Villanueva Siasoco, "Hard Labor, How Unions Fought to Honor the American Worker," Infoplease, www.infoplease.com.

9. "A Short History Of American Labor," *AFL-CIO American Federationist*, March 1981.

10. Larry Dewitt, "Brief History," SSA Historian's Office, Social Security Online, History, updated March 2003, www.ssa.gov.

11. Franklin D. Roosevelt, Message of the President to Congress, June 8, 1934, www.ssa.gov.

12. "The United States of America, Part Eight," International History Project, http://ragz-international.com.

13. Eric Lundquist, "What's Good for GM . . .," *Eweek*, June 23, 2003, www.eweek.com.

14. Steven Prokesch, "Remaking the American CEO," *The New York Times*, January 25, 1987.

15. William H. Whyte, *The Organization Man* (New York: Doubleday, 1956).

16. Candace Rich, "TV Variety shows," The Fifties Web, www.fiftiesweb.com.

17. Nina C. Leibman, "Comedy, Domestic Settings," www.museum.tv.

18. Martin Luther King, Jr., "I Have a Dream," August 28, 1963, in *Martin Luther King, Jr.: The Peaceful Warrior* (New York: Pocket Books, 1968).

19. "*Brown v. Board of Education*, Myths v. Truths," Brown Foundation for Educational Equity, Excellence, and Research, April 11, 2004, http://brownvboard.org.

20. "Death of Loyalty; The Price That Industry Pays for Downsizing/Downsizing Is Bad for Employee Loyalty," *The Economist (of London)/Buffalo (New York) News*, January 14, 1996.

21. Richard Reeves, "Loss of Work Is a Loss of Identity," *Buffalo (New York) News*, January 8, 1996.

22. Craig R. Taylor, "Focus on Talent Zoom In," *Business and Management Practices*.

23. Daniel McGinn, "Quitting Time: Companies Are Hiring Again, and Guess Who's Applying?" *Newsweek*, May 24, 2004.

Chapter 2

1. Jerry J. Jasinowski, "U.S. Faces Huge Shortage of Skilled Workers," Idea House, National Center For Policy Analysis, September 6, 1999, www.ncpa.org.

2. Kathy Sherbrooke, "Concierge Services Remain Strong," *Circles*, http://doit.circles.com.

3. Brandon Hall et al, "Top Training Priorities Survey," *Training Magazine*, February 1, 2004.

4. BLS Releases 2002-12, Employment Projections, February 11, 2004, Bureau of Labor Statistics, www.bls.gov.

5. Employment Policy Foundation, "Labor Day 2003: Annual Report Examines 150 Years of Realties, Challenges, and Opportunities in the Workplace," August 26, 2003, www.epf.org.

6. Cord Cooper, "Dealing With People Effectively: Bridging Generation Gaps," *Investors Business Daily*, July 31, 2003.

7. David Ellwood, "Grow Faster Together, or Grow Slowly Apart," Domestic Strategy Group, The Aspen Institute, www.aspeninstitute.org.

8. James T. Bond et al., "When Work Works, Summary of Families and Work Institute Research Findings," Families and Work Institute, http://familiesandwork.org.

9. "New Generation of Workers Has Different Views, Expectations," 2002 People at Work Survey, Mercer Human Resource Consulting LLC, July 16, 2003.

10. Craig R. Taylor et al, "A Company Is Known by the People It Keeps," presented at ASTD International Conference and Exposition, 2003.

11. Current Jobs and Future Options, AFL-CIO Working for America Institute, www.workingforamerica.org.

12. Cathy Healy, "A Business Perspective on Workplace Flexibility: When Work Works, An Employer Strategy for the 21st Century," Families and Work Institute.

13. Julie Cohen, "I/Os in the Know Offer Insights on Generation X Workers," *APA Monitor*, Vol. 33, no. 2, February 2002.

14. Cindy Simmons, "Review of Generation X," United Press International, January 25, 1992.

15. "More Mothers in the Labor Force This Mother's Day," Employment Policy Foundation, www.epf.org.

16. "What Labor Shortage? Debunking a Popular Myth, Wharton School of the University of Pennsylvania, August 27, 2003.

17. "Women in Retirement," EBRI Databook on Employee Benefits, 4th ed., 1997, and 2001 Retirement Confidence Survey, November 2001.

18. "Real Time with Bill Maher," HBO, January 23, 2004, broadcast transcript.

19. Alison Stein Wellner, "Segmenting Seniors," *Forecast*, March 2003.

20. "Backgrounder: Workforce Diversity: No Longer Just a Black and White Issue," The Changing Face of the 21st Century Workforce: Trends in Ethnicity, Race, Age, and Gender, The Employment Policy Foundation, www.epf.org.

21. Bureau of Labor Statistics, "Employee Tenure in 2002," September 19, 2002, www.bls.gov.

22. Dianne M. Durkin, "A Generation Gap Could Fracture Your Team: Don't Let It Happen," *Behavioral Health Management*, March/April 2004

23. "Adecco Survey Finds That Benefits Influence Retirees Aged 55–70 to Return To Work," March 1, 2001, www.business wire.com.

Chapter 3

1. Sue Shellenbarger, "Bumbling Managers Create Bruised Employee Loyalty," *Wall Street Journal Online*, www.career journal.com.

2. "Food Marketing Industry Speaks," *FMI*, 2003,www.fmi
.org; Lori Calabro, "Making Fares Fairer," *CFO*, September 1,
2002; Bob Swanson, "Are Labor Costs Masked by Inflation?"
NACS, August 2002.

3. "Mass Layoff Statistics," U.S. Department of Labor, www
.bls.gov.

4. Yuki Noguchi, "AT&T Plans More Cuts in Workforce,"
Washington Post, October 8, 2004.

5. Associated Press, "Bank of America to Cut 4,500 More
Jobs," *USA Today*, October 7, 2004.

6. "Analyst: SBC Gearing Up for Layoffs," *Houston Business
Journal*, November 5, 2004.

7. Eilene Zimmerman, "Why Deep Layoffs Hurt Long-Term
Recovery," *Workforce*, November 2001.

8. "The Metlife Study of Employee Benefits Trends" December 2003, www.metlife.com.

9. Patt Johnson/Gannett News Service, "Lifetime Employee
Loyalty Fades in Workplace," *Detroit News*, August 20, 2002.

10. "Walker Loyalty Report: Loyalty in the Workplace," September 2003.

11. David Myron, "The Loyalty Factor," *Destination CRM*,
October 28, 2003.

12. Katherine J. Sweetman, "Employee Loyalty Around the
Globe," *MIT Sloan Management Review*, Winter 2001, vol. 42, no.
2.

13. Matt Bloom, "Employee Loyalty Can't Be Purchased,"
HRM Guide, www.hrmguide.com.

14. Dianne M. Durkin, "Surveys, Customer Satisfaction, and
Increasing the Corporate Loyalty Factor," *Customer Interface Magazine*, March/April 2004.

15. Phil Zinkewicz, "Psych-101 for CSRs and Bottom Lines,"
Insurance Advocate, March 2002.

16. "Lifetime Value Analysis Puts Customer Loyalty Into Perspective," *The Ruf Report*, vol. 5, no. 1, 1997, www.ruf.com.

Chapter 4

1. Ronald G. Pantello, "Loyalty Matters in the Making of Corporate Culture," *MM&M*, August 1998.

2. Steven Greenhouse, "The Mood at Work: Anger and Anxiety," *The New York Times*, October 29, 2002.

3. Steven Greenhouse, "Looks Like a Recovery, Feels Like a Recession," *The New York Times*, September 1, 2003.

4. Adam Cohen, "What Studs Terkel's 'Working' Says About Worker Malaise Today," *New York Times,* May 31, 2004.

5. Douglas Smith, "Value Vs. Values: The Organizational Split," sample chapter courtesy of *Financial Times,* Prentice-Hall, June 4, 2004, www.informit.com.

6. William Safire, "The Crisis of Institutional Loyalty," *The New York Times*, August 18, 1986.

7. Dianne M. Durkin, "Business Leadership in 2002: Bringing Back the Basics: Trust, Respect, and Profit," HR.Com, March 2002.

8. James K. Harter, "Taking Feedback to the Bottom Line," *Gallup Management Journal*, March 15, 2001.

9. Walter Dill Scott, *Increasing Human Efficiency in Business: A Contribution to the Psychology of Business*, Electronic Text Center, University of Virginia Library, http://wyllie.lib.virginia.edu.

10. Controller's Report, "Turnover Rates," *Business and Management Practices*, October 2002.

11. William C. Symonds, "Staples: Riding High on Small Biz," *Business Week* online, April 5, 2004, www.businessweek.com.

12. Dean Foust et al., "Special Report—*Business Week* 50," *Business Week* online, April 5, 2004, www.businessweek.com.

13. Alison Overholt, "Flying With Fast Company, New Leaders, New Agenda," *American Way Magazine*, June 15, 2002.

14. William C. Symonds, "Thinking Outside the Big Box," *Business Week*, August 11, 2003.

15. "Intellectual Capital and Knowledge Management," *Chief Executive*, July 2001.

16. Andy Serwer, "Southwest Airlines: The Hottest Thing in the Sky," *Fortune*, February 23, 2004.

17. "About Southwest Airlines," www.southwest.com.

18. James R. Gregory, *The Best of Branding* (New York: McGraw-Hill, 2003).

19. Rich DiGeorgio, "Thought Leaders: Jackie Huba," www.hr.com.

20. Frank Reeves, "Now More Than Ever, in Tough Times, It's Crucial for Management to Be Open and Buttress Worker Morale," *Pittsburgh Post-Gazette*, April 8, 2003.

Chapter 5

1. Bureau of Labor Statistics, Organization for Economic Cooperation and Development, and Singapore Department of Statistics, charts 7, 10, 19, www.dol.gov.

2. Steven Greenhouse, "The Mood at Work: Anger and Anxiety," *The New York Times*, October 29, 2002.

3. David Creelman and Jay Weir, "A Conversation With Judy Walton," Reality HR, November 19, 2003, www.hr.com.

4. Mel Kleiman, "You've Got to Earn Employee Loyalty," *Tobacco Retailer*, August 2001, p. 35.

5. Gareth Morgan and Asaf Zohar, "Ricardo Semler's Transformation at Semco," *Imaginization*, www.imaginiz.com.

6. Brad Wieners, "Ricardo Semler: Set Them Free," *CIO/Insight*, April 1, 2004.

7. David Creelman, "Interview: Ricardo Semler on a New Form of Management," www.hr.com.

8. Craig R. Taylor, "Focus on Talent Zoom-In," *Business and Management Practices*, December 2002.

9. Tom Peters, "The Brand Called You," *Fast Company*, August/September 1997.

10. "About Eastern Bank," www.easternbank.com.

11. Ali Alemozafar, "Dell President Addresses Students," *The Stanford Daily*, April 23, 2003.

12. Brad Stone," At Dell, He's No Second Fiddle," *Newsweek*, February 23, 2004.

13. Robert Weisman, "Dell Aims to Put Fire Back Into Corporate Culture," *Boston Globe*, November 9, 2003.

14. Whitney Tilson, "The High Cost of Dell's Stock Option Program," thestreet.com, June 26, 2001.

15. Andrew Park et al, "What You Don't Know About Dell," *Business Week*, November 3, 2003.

16. "Reality HR: Paul Mckinnon, Dell," www.hr.com.

17. "Soul of Dell," Dell, www.us.del.com.

18. Robert Weisman, "A Push to Give Stakeholders Their Fair Share," *The Boston Globe*, November 23, 2003.

Chapter 6

1. Rosanne D'Ausilio, "The Human Touch Will Never Be Replaced," *Thinking Aloud*, May 24, 2004, www.imakenews.com.

2. Frederick Reichheld, *The Loyalty Effect* (Cambridge, MA: HBS Press, 1996).

3. Stuart Elliott, "New Survey on Ad Effectiveness," *The New York Times*, April 14, 2004.

4. Jean Chatzky, "Why More Women Are Buying Homes Alone," *Today*, July 9, 2004, http://msnbc.msn.com.

5. Jennifer Pittman, "Home Improvement Stores Helping Women Wield Their Tools," *Silicon Valley/San Jose Business Journal*, July 7, 2003.

6. "Lowe's Holds Annual Meeting of Shareholders," May 28, 2004, Prnewswire-Firstcall.

7. Andrea Coombes, "Gender Gap," *Women's Wall Street,* July 7, 2004, www.womenswallstreet.com.

8. Larry Dignan, "Lowe's Big Plan," *Baseline,* June 16, 2003.

9. Harry R. Weber, Associated Press, "Home Depot Refocuses on Customer Service," *Deseret Morning News,* November 26, 2003.

10. Patricia Sellers, "Home Depot, Something to Prove," *Fortune,* June 27, 2002.

11. Greg Levine, "Nardelli: Home Depot CEO Confronts Lowe's Challenge," *Forbes,* June 16, 2004.

12. Kevin Hogan et al, *Selling Yourself to Others: The New Psychology of Sales,* Pelican, 2002.

13. Jonathan Pont, "Loyalty Matters," *Potentials,* May 1, 2004.

14. Alison Overholt, "Cuckoo for Customers," *Fast Company,* June 2004.

15. Rackspace, www.rackspace.com.

16. "Frost & Sullivan Honors Rackspace for Customer Service," *San Antonio Business Journal,* July 21, 2003.

17. Om Malik, "How the Smallest Survive," *Business 2.0,* April 2004.

18. James Aldridge, "Rackspace's Year-End Revenues up 48 Percent for 2003," *San Antonio Business Journal,* February 17, 2004.

19. "Best Buy Accelerates Customer Centricity Transformation," News Release, Best Buy, May 3, 2004, www.bestbuy.com.

20. Parija Bhatnagar, "Best Buy's 'Geek Squad' to the Rescue," *CNN/Money,* June 16, 2004.

21. Benno Groeneveld, "Best Buy Joins Forces With Geek Squad," *The Business Journal* (Minneapolis/St. Paul), October 24, 2002.

22. Michelle Higgins, "Latest Retail Offer: Geeks on Call," *Wall Street Journal,* May 20, 2004.

23. Amey Stone, "Shopping for Electronics, Peacefully," *Business Week* Online, December 9, 2003, www.businessweek.com.

24. Steve Smith, "A Reporter's View of Best Buy's 'Consumer Centricity' Strategy, *Twice*, May 17, 2004.

Chapter 7

1. Rich DiGeorgio, "Thought Leaders: Jackie Huba," www.hr.com.

2. "KitchenAid," www.forum.kitchenaid.com.

3. Chuck Martin, "Power to the Employees," *Darwin*, March 2004.

4. Linda Tischler, "How Do I Love Thee," *Fast Company*, July 2004.

5. Matthew Patsky, "Healthy-Living Stocks for High Returns," *Forbes*, May 26, 2004.

6. Charles Fishman, "The Anarchist's Cookbook," *Fast Company*, July 2004.

7. "Declaration of Interdependence," Whole Foods Market, www.wholefoodsmarket.com.

8. "For Seventh Straight Year, Whole Foods Market Team Members Place Company on '100 Best Companies to Work For' List," January 6, 2004, www.wholefoodsmarket.com.

9. "Whole Foods Market Named to *Child* Magazine's First-Ever 10 Top Family-Friendly Supermarket Chains List," Whole Foods Market, July 27, 2003, www.wholefoodsmarket.com.

10. "Whole Foods Market, the Best Supermarkets for Families," *Child*, www.child.com.

Chapter 8

1. "National Survey Finds Workers Starved for Information," Randstad North America, April 30, 2002.

2. William C. Taylor, "Companies Find They Can't Buy Love With Bargains," *New York Times*, August 8, 2004.

Chapter 9

1. Diane E. Lewis, "Work Force: Employers Keep Workers' Good Will," *The Boston Globe*, June 8, 2003.

2. Ivan Temes, "How to Turn Challenges Into Opportunities," Aspire Now, www.aspire.com.

3. Statistics from the Gallup Organization quoted on USDA web site, http://hr.ffas.usda.gov/offices/gallup/gallup.htm.

4. Jonathan Pont, "Loyalty Matters," *Potentials*, May 2004.

5. "Management Giant, Louis Frederick Gerstner," *Business: The Ultimate Resource*, (Bloomsbury Publishing Plc 2003), www.ultimatebusinessresource.com.

6. "New York Times: Reporter Routinely Faked Articles," CNN, May 11, 2003, www.cnn.com.

7. Alfred Lubrano et al., "Scandal Brings Down Times Editors," *Philadelphia Inquirer*, June 6, 2003, www.philly.com.

8. Lori Robertson, "Down With Top-Down," *AJR*, August/September 2003, www.ajr.org.

9. James R. Stengel, Andrea L. Dixon, Chris T. Allen, "Listening Begins at Home," *Harvard Business Review*, November 1, 2003.

Chapter 10

1. Bob Woods, "Harvesting Your Human Capital," *Chief Executive*, July 2001, www.chiefexecutive.net.

2. "The Sunday Times Top 100 Companies to Work For," Beaverbrooks, www.beaverbrooks.co.uk.

3. "Beaverbrooks, Jewelry Chain with a Heart of Gold," *Sunday Times*, March 7, 2004, http://business.timesonline.co.uk.

4. Thornburg Investment Management, Inc., "Holdings Commentary, IHOP Corporation (IHP)," www.thornburg investments.com.

5. Julie Connelly, "IHOP Stacks Up," *NYSE*, May 3, 2004, www.nyse.com.

6. "IHOP," www.ihop.com.

7. "Research Studies: Peoplebrand: The Employment Brand Imperative," www.right.com.

Chapter 11

1. "Right Now On NYSE.Com," *NYSE*, May/June 2004, p. 9.

2. "Towers Perrin Survey Finds Almost Half of American Workers Doubt the Credibility of Employer Communications," The Corporate Social Responsibility Newswire Service, January 7, 2004, www.csrwire.com.

3. "Look Who's Listening!" Randstad North America, July 8, 2003, www.us.randstad.com.

4. "Planetree Focus Is on Giving Patients What They Want," *AHA News*, September 8, 2003, www.hospitalconnect.com.

5. "Cultural Practices of the Best Companies," Credibility Communication, Health Care/Hospital, Griffin Hospital," www .greatplacetowork.com.

6. "About Griffin Hospital," www.griffinhealth.org.

7. "Griffin Hospital Celebrates Fifth Anniversary on Fortune 'Best Places to Work For' List," December 29, 2003, www.griffin health.org.

8. J. P. Liebeskind, "Knowledge, Strategy, and the Theory of the Firm," *Strategic Management Journal*, Winter 1996, p. 93, http://socrates.berkeley.edu/~iir/cohre/liebeskind.html.

9. Phil Zinkewicz, "Psych-101 for CSRs and Bottom Lines," *Insurance Advocate*, March 2002.

10. Aaron Donovan, "Hello, Tech Support? I Need a Hug," *New York Times*, September 13, 2001.

11. Lou Hirsh, "Customer Service: The Inside Story on Customer Loyalty," *CRM Daily*, April 8, 2002.

12. Dave Patel, "Create Productive Customer Service Employees," Society for Human Resource Management, www.shrm.org.

Chapter 12

1. "The International," www.theinternational.com.

2. Jennifer Zaino, "Employee Collaboration on the Upswing," *Informationweek*, February 11, 2002, www.informationweek.com.

3. Waitsfield, Vermont, www.city-data.com/city/waitsfield-vermont.html.

4. Green Mountain Coffee Roasters, www.greenmountaincoffee.com.

5. Virginia Lindaur Simmon, "Java Man," *Vermont Guides*, February 2, 2003, www.vermontguides.com.

6. Katherine Austinson, "Green Mountain Coffee," *Coffee Connoisseurs*, April 29, 2003.

7. "Principle Profits Company Listings, Green Mountain Coffee Roasters (GMCR)," www.socialfunds.com.

8. Mark Pendergast, "Green Mountain Coffee Roasters: Doing Well by Doing Good," *Tea & Coffee*, April/May 2004, www.teaandcoffee.net.

Chapter 13

1. "Kronos Receives Top Honors for Exemplary Customer Satisfaction," March 8, 2004, Business Wire, http://phx.corporate-ir.net.

2. "Kronos Reports Third Quarter Fiscal 2004 Results; Revenue up 17 Percent on Strong Demand for Workforce Central 5," July 27, 2004, *Business Wire*, http://phx.corporate-ir.net.

3. "Kronos® Raises the Bar," July 13, 2004, www.kronos.com.

4. "About Kronos," www.kronos.com.

5. Orlen Grunewald et al., "Chickens in the Feedlot: The Tyson-IBP Merger," www.agecon.ksu.edu.

6. Nell Newton, "Tyson Foods, Inc., Factsheet," www.hoovers.com.

7. "Reality HR: Ken Kimbro, Tyson Foods—a Billion Dollar Business," www.hr.com.

8. "Sodexho USA Honors Kellogg's, Tyson Food, American Express, and Sweet Street With 2003 Vendor of the Year Awards," June 23, 2003, Sodexho USA, www.sodexhousa.com.

9. Ante Pulic, "Intellectual Capital—Does It Create or Destroy Value?" *Measuring Business Excellence*, vol. 8, no. 1, 2004, p. 62, as found on http://iris.emeraldinsight.com.

Chapter 14

1. Chuck Lucier et al, "CEO Succession 2003: The Perils of 'Good Governance,'" *Strategy + Business*, Issue 35, Summer 2004, published by Booz Allen Hamilton, www.straategy + business.com.

2. "Most Employees Feel Trust and Loyalty for Their Corporate Leaders Says New SHRM/Careerjournal.Com Poll," July 26, 2004, www.careerjournal.com.

3. Bob Woods, "Q&A, James E. Copeland, Jr., Chief Executive Officer of Deloitte Touche Tohmatsu," *Chief Executive*, July 2001.

4. Diane E. Lewis, "Survey Forecasts Focus on Recruitment," *The Boston Globe*, January 4, 2004.

5. "Lessons in Leadership With Roger Nierenberg," *The Daily Leader*, December 9, 2002, www.themusicparadigm.com.

6. John Heider, *The Tao of Leadership*, Bantam Books, 1985, p. 135.

7. "Texas Turnaround," *Business Week* online, January 10, 2000, www.businessweek.com.

8. Paul Harris, "Case Study: BTS Helps Companies Walk in Customers' Shoes," *Learning Circuits*, June 2004, www.learning circuits.org.

9. Robert Celaschi, "A Simulation That Makes Employees Feel Customer Pain," *Workforce Management*, August 2004.

10. Michelle Conlin, "The Big Squeeze on Workers," *Business Week Online*, May 13, 2002, www.businessweek.com.

11. Scott Miller, "How to Build Loyalty Before the Employee Shortage Hits," *Entrepreneur*, July 8, 2002.

12. "Texas Instruments Factsheet," www.hoovers.com.

13. "Texas Instruments, 2004 America's Most Admired Companies," *Fortune*, March 8, 2004, www.fortune.com.

14. Frances Hesselbein, "A Time for Leaders," *Leader to Leader*, Winter 2002, pp. 4-6.

15. "Abraham Maslow Biography—Hierarchy of Needs Framework," *Value Based Management*, www.valuebased management.net.

16. Kathleen Landis, "Blue Sky Thinking," *MyBusiness*, June/July 2003, www.nfib.com.

17. U.S. Small Business Administration, FAQ, http://app1.sba.gov/faqs.

18. "Celeste Volz Ford, Biography," www.stellarsolutions.com.

19. "Stellar Solutions, Inc.," 2002 Winning Workplaces, www.winningworkplaces.org.

20. Julie Sloane, "The Iconoclast: Celeste Ford; The Best Bosses," *Fortune*, October 2003.

Chapter 15

1. Alan Rowe, *Creative Intelligence, Leadership, and the Challenge of the Future*, May 28, 2004, sample chapter courtesy of *Financial Times*, Prentice-Hall, www.informit.com.

2. "An Overall Approach to Change Management," Booz Allen Hamilton, July 7, 2004, www.boozallen.com.

3. Lori Robertson, "Down With Top-Down," *AJR*, August/September 2003, www.ajr.org.

4. Daniel Goleman, "Leading Resonant Teams," *Leader to Leader*, 25 (Summer 2002), pp. 24-30.

5. Frances Hesselbein, "A Time for Leaders," *Leader to Leader*, 23 (Winter 2002), pp. 4-6.

6. Saj-nicole A. Joni, "The Geography of Trust," *Harvard Business Review*, March 1, 2004.

7. "About Keyspan," www.keyspanenergy.com.

8. Anne Law, "Keyspan Corporation," www.hoovers.com.

9. "Reality HR: Kenny Moore, Contradiction of Leadership," www.hr.com.

10. Robert B. Catell, Kenny Moore, and Glenn Rifkin, "Cool Friends: Kenny Moore," www.tompeters.com.

11. Linda Tischler, "Kenny Moore Held a Funeral and Everyone Came," *Fast Company*, February 2004.

12. "Keyspan Energizes Its Web Presence with Interwoven and Agency.Com," Case Study, Interwoven, Inc.

13. "Keyspan Tops Customer Satisfaction Survey," www.keyspanenergy.com.

14. "Charles Lewis Tiffany Biography," www.tiffany.com.

15. Elizabeth Cornell, "Tiffany & Co. Factsheet," www.hoovers.com.

16. Tiffany & Co., 2003 Annual Report.

17. "Victoria Berger-Gross, First Person Tearsheet," www.forbes.com.

18. "Reality HR: Victoria Berger-Gross on Culture Change," www.hr.com.

Chapter 16

1. U.S. Department of Homeland Security, "Remarks by Secretary of Homeland Security Tom Ridge Regarding Recent Threat Reports," August 1, 2004, www.dhs.gov.

2. Edward Rappaport, "Terrorism: The New Occupational Hazard," CRS Report for Congress, Congressional Research Service, The Library Of Congress, March 29, 2002.

3. U.S. Department of State, Office of the Coordinator for Counterterrorism, "Patterns of Global Terrorism, 2002," Appendix H, Statistical Review, April 30, 2003, www.state.gov.

4. Thomas J. Lueck et al., "New York Cites a Terror Threat," *The New York Times*, August 1, 2004.

5. Nikola Krastev, "U.S.: New Yorkers Alert, but Calm, After New Specific Threats," Radio Free Europe, August 3, 2004, www.rferl.org.

6. Manuel Roig-Franzia, "Hurricane Charley Tears Across Fla.," *Washington Post*, August 13, 2004; John Copenhaver, "Small Businesses Could Be Among Charley's Casualties," *The Tampa Tribune*, August 17, 2004; "Hurricane Charley Blamed for 25th Florida Death," CNN, August 21, 2004, www.cnn.com.

7. Daintry Duffy, "Practice Makes Perfect," *CSO*, November 2002.

8. "USAA Named to Computerworld's List of Best Places to Work in IT," July 2, 2004, https://www.gc.usaa.com; "Who We Are," https://www.gc.usaa.com; "USAA a Top 10 Military Friendly Employer," January 9, 2004, https://www.gc.usaa.com; "USAA Rated No. 1 In Customer Advocacy," August 6, 2004, https://www.gc.usaa.com.

9. "USAA Factsheet," www.hoovers.com.

10. Scott Berinato, "All Systems Down," *CIO*, February 15, 2003.

11. Anne Barnard, "Got Paper? Beth Israel Deaconess Copes with a Massive Computer Crash," *The Boston Globe*, November 26, 2002.

12. "2004 E-Crime Watch Survey Shows Significant Increase in Electronic Crimes," *CSO*, May 25, 2004; data originating from *CSO* magazine/U.S. Secret Service/CERT Coordination Center, www.cert.org/about/ecrime.html.

13. Michele Kurtz, "His Goal: Computerized Patient Records," *The Boston Globe*, August 24, 2004.

14. "BIDMC Cited as Model for Commitment to Change and Innovation in Patient Care Delivery," Beth Israel Deaconess Medical Center, August 24, 2004, www.bidmc.harvard.edu.

15. Lori Robertson, "Down With Top-Down," *AJR*, August/September 2003, www.ajr.org.

Chapter 17

1. C. Bartlett and S. Ghoshal. "Changing the Role of the Top Management: Beyond Systems to People," *Harvard Business Review*, May-June 1995.

2. "Graniterock Team Named to *Fortune* 'Best Bosses,'" www.graniterock.com.

3. Nancy K. Austin, "Rock Through the Ages," *Inc.*, May 2000.

4. "About Us," Graniterock, www.graniterock.com.

5. "Granite Rock: A Case Study in Quality," *Masonry*, October 2002.

6. "Fun Companies: Granite Rock," *Graduating Engineer*.

7. Bob Woods, "Harvesting Your Human Capital," *Chief Executive*, July 2001.

8. Charles Fishman, "A Dose of Change," *Fast Company*, August 2001.

9. Leadership Forum, "Leadership Example," posted by MLOGS at July 18, 2004, www.managementlogs.com.

10. "2004 Best Companies to Work For: Amgen," *Fortune*, January 12, 2004.

11. "Amgen, Profile," www.biospace.com.

12. "2004 Cambridge-Boston Recipients of Amgen Award for Science Teaching Excellence Announced," News Release, April 28, 2004, www.amgen.com.

13. Arlene Weintraub, "Amgen Opens the Secret Curtain," *Business Week*, March 22, 2004.

14. Jeff Swartz, "Doing Well and Doing Good: The Business Community and National Service," *Brookings Review*, Fall 2002, vol. 20, no. 4, pp. 23-24; and "About Timberland," www.timber land.com.

15. "4,500 Volunteers Worldwide to Perform Equivalent of 3.5 Years of Non-Stop Community Service in a Single Day," The Timberland Company, October 2, 2003, www.timberland.com.

16. "People, Planet, Profit: The Value of Corporate Social Responsibility," *EORM's Quarterly E-Zine*, edition no. 8, www .eorm.com.

17. Katherine J. Sweetman, "Employee Loyalty Around the Globe," MIT Sloan Management Review, Winter 2001, vol. 42, no.2, p. 16.

18. "New Poll Shows Most Employees Feel Trust and Loyalty for Their Corporate Leaders," July 26, 2004, www.shrm.org.

19. "The Timberland Company Selected by Industry Week Magazine as One of the 50 Best Manufacturing Companies," The Timberland Company, August 13, 2004, www.timberland.com.

20. "Doing Good Makes Staff More Loyal," *The New York Times,* July 13, 2003; and "Fast Facts," The Timberland Company, www.timberland.com.

Index

About the Author

Dianne Durkin is the president and founder of Loyalty Factor, a consulting and training company that enhances employee, customer, and brand loyalty for some of the nation's most prominent corporations and smaller businesses. She has more than twenty-five years of experience in training and development, finance, direct sales, and international marketing, and is widely recognized as a visionary thinker, who, with a rare combination of creativity and a strong business sense, can take abstract ideas and turn them into reality. Quick to get to the core issues within a company and outline their impact on the organization and its profits, productivity, and people, she is continually sought after to lead companies into new markets and in new directions, handle organizational restructures, and set up programs that will build lasting commitments with employees and customers.

Durkin has been interviewed by National Public Radio and Bloomberg Television & Radio and featured in the *New York Times, Wall Street Journal, Fortune, USA Today, Investor's Business Daily,* and the *Boston Globe,* among numerous other publications, and was the subject of a cover story in *Learning and Training* magazine.

A graduate of Rivier College, Durkin holds a master's degree from Duquesne University and has completed advanced programs at the University of Santa Clara and Babson College. She is active in the Boston Club, Commonwealth Institute, the CEO Club, Who's Who in America, and Women in World Trade.